TheKnowledge

Digital Strategy in Culture

by Art of Digital London

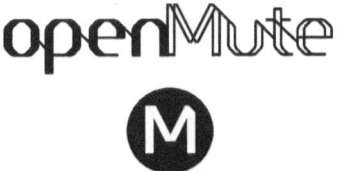

TheKnowledge - Digital Strategy in Culture
By Art of Digital London

Part of TheKnowledge, a wiki for the sharing of digital skills between cultural workers http://theknowledge.aodl.org.uk/

Join us at our monthly Meetup http://www.meetup.com/art-of-digital-london

Published by OpenMute Press, a Mute Publishing imprint, 46 Lexington St., London W1F 0LP

Contact us: @aodl | mute@metamute.org | 00 44 (0)20 3287 9005

Except for the images, which originally appeared elsewhere and are republished here, all content is copyright of Mute Publishing. However, Mute Publishing encourages use of its content for purposes that are non-commercial, critical, or disruptive of capitalist property relations. Please make sure you credit Mute Publishing as the original publisher.

This legend is devised in the absence of a licence which adequately represents this book's contributors' respective position on copyright, and to acknowledge but deny the copyrighting performed by default where copyright is waived.

Project director: Simon Worthington
Project assistant: Caroline Heron
Copy author: Paul Squires, Perera
Copy editor: Paul Graham
Managing editor: Pauline van Mourik Broekman
Design production, print and web: Raquel Perez de Eulate, OpenMute

MediaWiki configuration: Michiel van der Haagen
eBook layout Tom Clark

eBook conversion by Mute's own eBook engine, Progressive Publishing System http://theknowledge.aodl.org.uk/index.php/PPS

Available as EBook ISBN: 978-1-906496-69-2
ISBN: 978-1-906496-68-5
Published 2012

Supported by Arts Council England

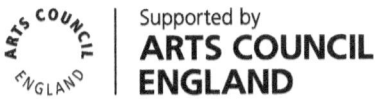

Contents

About TheKnowledge — 10
A time of transition — 11
   People at TheKnowledge — 13
   'Art of Digital London: Digital Salon & Surgeries' — 14

Chapter 1 Publishing
Say goodbye to dusty store rooms full of unsold books! 16

   Publishing platforms — 18
      E-books — 18
         Amazon Kindle — 20
         Apple iBooks — 22
         Example: Artists' eBooks — 23
      Apps and HTML5 — 24
         Example: PugPig — 25
      Print On Demand (POD), including short run printing — 26
         Example: Don't Panic: Organise! — 28
   Some more practical considerations — 30
         Example: O/R Books — 31
   Copyright — 32
   The future — 36

Chapter 2 Video
A new era of public service publishing? 38

Cameras, filming and post-production	39
Example: One & Other	40
Content	42
Example: Deptford.TV	43
Example: Sadler's Wells	44
Example: Philharmonia Orchestra	45
Distribution	47
Example: Tate Channel	49
Example: Institute of Contemporary Arts	50
Example: VisionOn.TV	51
A word about selling and marketing your content	52
Example: MUBI Europe	53

Chapter 3 Archiving
Avoiding digital dodos, keeping your work in circulation 56

Developing a digital archive	59
Example: National Portfolio Organisation archives	59
Cloud storage	60
Databases	61
Adding content	63
Example: Theatricalia – an audiences' archive	64
Access and Security	66

Chapter 4 Open Source
The where, why, what and who!........... 68

What is open source?	69
Why has open source become popular?	69
Has open source been successful?	70
Example: Goto10	70
Finding open source software	72
Example: PAD.MA (Public Access Digital Media Archive)	72
SourceForge	73
Launchpad	73
Savannah	73
Free Software Directory	74
GitHub	74
Google Code and CodePlex	74
Intellectual property	75
Examples of open source licence types	75
GPL (GNU Public Licence)	75
BSD license (Berkeley Software Distribution)	76
EUPL (European Union Public Licence)	76
MIT Licence	77
Material licencing	77
Participating in open source communities	78
Example: Open Source Publishing (OSP)	80
Open source and your digital work	81
Open source and your non-digital work	81

Chapter 5 Audio
Catching butterflies with copyright nets 84

Audio on the internet	85
Example: London Sinfonietta	88
Example: Chord Punch	89
Digital audio production	90
Example: Ogg Vorbis	92
Recording audio	94
Music	94
Speech	94
Theatrical performance	94
Presenting your digital audio	95
Internet radio	95
Publicising your audio	96
Example: Backdoor Broadcasting Company	97
Commercial models	98
Example: NMC Recordings & State51's Greedbag	99

Chapter 6 Gaming
Gaming as learning, gaming as culture, gaming as a new context....................................102

Example: Chromaroma	103
Artistic projects	106
Example: Warmail	108
Marketing campaigns	109
Education and Outreach programmes	110
Example: Tate Kids	111

Chapter 7 Community and Social Media
Opening the door to dynamic audiences 112

A potted history	113
What are online communities good for?	114
Some more issues to consider	116
Managing communities, managing openness	118
Identifying, building and retaining an audience	121

About TheKnowledge

TheKnowledge lends its name from the London cab drivers' examination, which tests future cabbies' navigation skills in the streets of London. Drivers internalise London's idiosyncratic street network by memorising hundreds of 'runs', moving endlessly around the city streets until knowledge of them is etched indelibly in their memory.

With this online environment, TheKnowledge, we've wanted to evoke that sense that learning happens by doing. Moreover, that it is from other practitioners, implementing tools and approaches in practical situations, that those new to something often learn the most. We've called this process peer learning, and it is intended to reflect the experiences of practitioners working in organisations of all sizes, as they tackle a variety of issues in artistic and operational development. We have compiled the research we conducted in a collaborative writing platform, a Wiki, not only to aide us in the collective collation of material, but to signal a hope that this work can continue on such a collective basis.

TheKnowledge publishes guides to:

- Publishing
- Video
- Archiving
- Open Source
- Audio
- Gaming
- Community and Social Media

TheKnowledge sits under the umbrella of Art of Digital London (AoDL), which runs regular social events, training sessions and meetings about digital strategy in culture. The project has been organised by OpenMute, Mute Publishing's sister agency, which possesses decades of experience analysing the net and developing open source software. Having grown up with the free culture movements associated with the nascent, critical net culture of the 1990s and 2000s, OpenMute's initiatives advocate for an open net. This means open standards and non-proprietary systems; working in collaborative communities; the net as place of heterogeneous voices; and many to many media. Most importantly, it means seeing the net as a place where productive artistic, social and political reconfigurations occur.

A time of transition

As society is altered by ever expanding digital networks, cultural organisations have to grapple with a world in transition. Media are under fundamental transformation, with photography moving from chemical and paper to screens and metadata, 'the internet of things' ushering augmented reality into the white cube, and the mass audiences of television and film splintering into a thousands niches.

In addressing this condition of digital transition the following key issues continue to inflect our research topics:

- **The public domain:** there is a struggle to maintain a public domain on the net, where pluralism is valued and artistic experimentation can be supported. The threat of the ground (or 'real estate') of the net becoming privately owned is ever-present.
- **Economic models:** Promises come and go, net gurus and commercial media pundits can't help

but promise the earth. Remember 'the long tail', a principle of web distribution which was going to help small producers win out? Well, it proved to be quite the opposite: the long tail turned out to be that of digital labour (as theorised by Trebor Scholz), benefiting primarily big players like Google, while smaller players remain perilously ill-equipped to bring incomes and content provision – still expected to be free – into some kind of balance. As cultural organisations and individual media makers, our audiences may double and triple, but reliable economic models remain thin on the ground.

- **Organisational change:** integrating the net into artistic and operational practice means root and branch changes for many organisations. There are processes of disintermediation and disruption to adapt to; artistic areas – like photography – have become almost fully digital, while supply chains have moved almost entirely online. These challenges must often be understood outside of traditional IT contexts; to make the right decisions on digital strategy, all areas of an organisation should be involved.
- **Different stories:** the cultural sector has a different set of orientations than the commercial, market led, media sector. Yet most of what we hear about the net is determined by the latter's agendas, meaning it can be hard to find more appropriate stories of good practice on the web.
- **Privacy and surveillance:** people's online lives are increasingly being tracked for commercial purposes. It is important to engage with these issues when working with social networks, ecommerce systems or locative media, as they have a significant bearing on civil liberties and freedom of expression.

- **Labour and value fluency:** understanding the value of our content and our relationships to our communities, creators and audiences. People's 'social graphs' – a term used to describe individuals' cumulative traces in social networks (through communication, browsing or purchasing activity) – create value. As your content is channelled through networks that create none of their own, it must be asked whether there is a fair trade-off between infrastructure provider and user activity?
- **Audiences are on the move:** you might think the directly experienced live event is impervious to the kinds of transformations digital networks are visiting upon other cultural forms. But even there, the opposite is true, as the alchemical reaction between authentic presence and socialised distribution continues to dramatically grow audiences for performers and their commissioners.

People at TheKnowledge

Simon Worthington – Director of digital, Mute Publishing
Caroline Heron – Project coordinator, Mute Publishing
Pauline van Mourik Broekman – Director, Mute Publishing

Research interns
Rosa Barney
Michael Conte
Keith Hubbard
Lauren Irizarry
Mamiko Nakano
Vanessa D'amico

'Art of Digital London: Digital Salon & Surgeries'

The Art of Digital London (AoDL) programme was initiated to facilitate the establishment and maintenance of a London RFO network investigating the relationship between art organisations and digital technology. The project began in September 2009 with a series of ten 'Digital Salon & Surgeries' – day long events where London arts administrators and producers, business and media consultants, developers, innovators and funders gathered together for conversations and show and tells. Recurring topics were the relationship between arts and technology communities and the evolving tool set used in the creation, production, distribution and marketing of artistic programmes. Through these events a comprehensive picture of the problems and benefits of digital media was developed. The events were administered through a ning social network (now closed) and the programme finished in November 2010. Art of Digital London: Salon & Surgeries was funded by Arts Council England, London, within the Digital Opportunities scheme. The programme was organised by OpenMute and IT4Arts of The Worshipful Company of Information Technologists (WCIT).

> http://theknowledge.aodl.org.uk/index.php/Digital_Salon_and_Surgeries

1
Publishing

Say goodbye to dusty store rooms full of unsold books!

Digital publishing, or electronic publishing, is the process by which text and images are sent to electronic media. The growth of digital publishing has been powered by shrinking costs and greater online access. Basically, it is cheaper than ever before to publish professional work, and to make it available to a wide range of audiences, thus opening new income streams. And because work is more widely available, it also offers greater and more sustained dialogue between producers, cultural organisations and audiences. It is now possible to publish information or artistic works frequently, with depth, and offering a two-way dialogue.

Digital content can be accessible from anywhere in the world, at any time and via a number of sources. E-books, for example, can be offered through a large and diverse number of retailers, which exponentially increases the availability of the work, and thus (potentially at least) its sales opportunities. In theory, digital publishing offers a chance for anyone to gain visibility on the global stage, from an individual at a kitchen table to book commissioners at the largest art institutions. What matters is the quality, frequency, and timeliness of the content available – as well as making it easy and attractive to buy. Achieving this is clearly a question of resources, but the opportunity remains there for smaller producers to punch above their weight.

With the rapid increase in web-connected devices – including mobiles, laptops and tablets – digital content has undergone something of a re-examination since the years of slow connections, chunky PCs and degraded and fractured rich media content. Producers of any size can benefit from this. The opportunities have never been greater to offer original work, delivered in the right way, to an audience that understands the contexts, limitations, and opportunities presented by the networked environment. These opportunities are not difficult to realise, although they require careful planning and a full understanding of your current audience – and how they wish to interact.

Publishing platforms

There are three different product types in which to publish your digital content. In the first two, the content remains in a digital format for the purposes of consumption. These are e-books (electronic books) and the more sophisticated, interactive productions which are available within HTML5 and apps. In the third example, Print On Demand (POD) publishing, digital technology offers a more flexible process, but the end result is still a physical book.

E-books

E-books are essentially equivalent to printed books, only in digital form. The content can be read directly from a computer or via specifically designed hardware called e-readers. Preparing content for publication as an e-book depends upon the medium through which it will be read, but a popular format is EPUB.

EPUB is a free and open e-book standard from the International Digital Publishing Forum. Books that use this format can be read on a wide variety of devices. The latest version of EPUB is version 3 (EPUB 3), which offers an even greater potential for published work. EPUB 3 documents can include rich media and interactivity, a wider choice of languages, and improved metadata, where publishers and authors can attach pertinent information relating to the origin of the content. Version 3 also supports CSS3, an additional markup language which caters for typography in different languages and characters. It is important to bear in mind, however, that EPUB 3-ready devices and software are only recently starting to appear.

You may therefore wish to offer your publication in an older version of EPUB for a broad audience, and offer a special EPUB 3 variant for those devices that can take advantage of the new developments.

> International Digital Publishing Forum – EPUB 3 specifications
> http://idpf.org/epub/30

There are many software tools which enable the production of EPUB files from source documents in various formats, including Microsoft Word, OpenOffice and HTML (the Web's markup language). EPUB is itself a markup language, in that the content of an EPUB file is 'marked up' with formats and other information. This also makes it quite easy to learn, should you be interested in knowing how to make EPUB files from scratch, or how to refine existing files.

You don't necessarily need to offer EPUB files through publishers or aggregators. You could simply offer an EPUB file for download from your website. There are many tools to read EPUB documents on a computer. This means that the level of variation is not dissimilar to website development, where ensuring compatibility with a variety of web browsers is vital for building and developing an audience. The advantage of the EPUB format is that it is an open, industry standard. Many retailers such as the Apple iBookstore will accept EPUB files to sell, and many devices (iOS devices, Sony Reader) will read them. The conspicuous exception here is the Amazon Kindle, which will not accept them. Therefore, to maximise reach, it may be necessary to blend EPUB with other formats.

Amazon Kindle

The Kindle is Amazon's device for reading books, magazines, and blogs and occupies the dominant position within the e-book market. It comes with a keyboard, is monochrome only, and has a direct hook into Amazon's online service. Therefore, consumers will need to register for an Amazon account before they can use a Kindle.

There are a number of ways to create an e-book for the Kindle. It accepts popular file formats including Word (.doc) and text (.txt). Amazon's guide to e-book creation from Word can help with getting through it. It also accepts HTML in zip form (.zip) and a format for 'native' electronic publishing work. PDFs are also accepted, but are not recommended due to their complexity. As mentioned, it does not accept the EPUB format.

> Amazon's guide to e-book
> http://forums.kindledirectpublishing.com/kdpforums/entry.jspa?externalID=553&categoryID=7

In order to publish to Kindle, you need to create a Kindle Direct Publishing (KDP) account, although if you already have an Amazon account, then you can use KDP from there. Log in to Amazon KDP. Click 'Add a new title', and follow the steps. You will need to consider pricing and royalty regulations, so read Amazon's pricing and royalty guide before starting.

> Amazon Kindle Direct Publishing
> http://kdp.amazon.com/

> Amazon pricing and royalty guide
> https://kdp.amazon.com/self-publishing/help?topicId=A29FL26OKE7R7B

Formatting and publishing your document can be undertaken within KDP. However, some users of Amazon KDP have implied that it is not as easy as it looks. The native file format for the Kindle is AZW, which – so it is suggested – is best produced from HTML. So, if you can produce your work for HTML first, you might be saving time and hassle.

Publishing magazines and blogs requires a different process to making a book. You will need to request to become a beta publisher, and Amazon has to approve you, which normally takes 24 hours.

Amazon Beta Publisher Program
https://kindlepublishing.amazon.com/gp/vendor/kindlepubs/kpp/kpp-home?*Version*=1&ie=UTF8&*entries*=0

Amazon requires certain information from you as part of this process.

1. Publication details, such as the publication's title, publisher's name, and publication type
2. An image to display in the Kindle store, usually a cover image
3. A product description, which will be displayed to customers in the online Kindle store
4. Masthead image – the title logo image
5. XML feeds – your publication content in XML: specifically, RSS2.0, NITF or XHTML format (most blogs automatically provide RSS 2.0). The feed must be full-fat (full text and images)
6. Contact details
7. Publishing frequency
8. Pricing details – for magazines, this is the revenue minus delivery costs x 70%, where the delivery costs are dependent on file size and a complex set of further variables. Bloggers receive 30% of

the gross revenue. See: https://kindlepublishing.amazon.com/gp/vendor/kindlepubs/common/get-content?id=200492750#RSTC4

For books, you can choose a royalty rate of 35% and 70% for selected territories. You then have delivery and tax deducted from this royalty. For example, in the UK, 20% sales tax is deducted. You can then enable price-match, where your sales price gets pegged to the lowest competitor price for the digital book, but obviously this is a dangerous game to play...

Expect to wait a month from the start of this process until your work ends up in the Kindle store.

Apple iBooks

iBooks are what Apple calls 'published works' and they are managed through the iBookstore, which is to books what iTunes is to music. Although in the media much of the focus has been on iPad apps (individual applications), it is possible and relatively easy to get your work into the iBookstore through the iBook submission form. Services called iBooks aggregators, which hold works on behalf of Apple, are available and can often be the quickest route to getting your work into iBooks. The downside is that the aggregator takes a cut, which can be around 50 to 60 per cent.

> iBook submission form
> https://itunesconnect.apple.com/WebObjects/iTunesConnect.woa/wa/apply

> iBook aggregators
> http://www.copyblogger.com/publish-in-ibookstore/

iBooks is available for all iOS devices, meaning that your work will be available through the iPhone and the iPad.

Submitting to iBooks takes more work than to the Kindle store. You will need:

1. An ISBN-13 number.
2. A US tax ID. This can be arranged through the IRS (the equivalent of the HMRC in the UK) and shouldn't take long.
3. The ability to upload EPUB files which are compliant with EpubCheck 1.0.5.

Artists' eBooks

Artists' eBooks is a project by James Brindle of booktwo. org, which explores the possibilities of e-book platforms specifically for art books. Through Artists' eBooks James seeks to develop partnerships with writers, artists, publishers, galleries and organisations that are interested in developing experimental new ways to incorporate audio, video, text and images into their publications. Guides and resources are also available through the site for those who would like to publish onto e-book platforms independently.

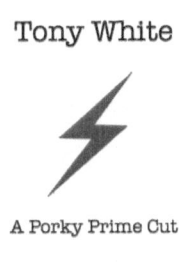

Image: A Porky Prime Cut, Tony White

> Authors such as Tony White and Kenji Siratori have already produced a series of new titles in collaboration with Artists' eBooks, which are freely available via the site in a range of eBook formats. Niven Govinden's new *L'histoire de Bexhill Baudelaire* is an example where the format has gone a little further in bringing in other media, e.g. a soundtrack has been incorporated into the text through a series of YouTube videos.
>
> http://www.artistsebooks.org/

Apps and HTML5

Apps (applications) are small software programs which undertake a specific function. Many books are available as apps, as apps allow for a greater level of interactivity, and can use specific functionality from the device, such as a camera or GPS. They can be much more expensive to develop (although the cost varies widely), but revenues generated from an app, if it is popular, can be significant.

There are many reasons as to why publishers have opted for apps. Commercially, they can be sold through 'app stores'. Formerly the exclusive domain of tablets, app stores are now becoming available on domestic computers, meaning that useful and interesting work can now attract a wider audience. However, it is also the level of sophistication inherent in apps that make them so appealing. When considering turning your work into an app, think about how your work can be made into something richer, with a greater level of multimedia content, and more interactive.

Such a level of sophistication is also becoming possible in HTML5, which is the latest version of HTML – the markup language that tells the browser how to display a web page. HTML has come a long way in a short space of time, and the level of interactivity now available in a web page is way beyond what was possible just ten years ago.

HTML5 offers a level of interactivity which is broadly consistent with an app. It even offers location awareness and, for the first time, the ability to play audio and video straight from the web browser, without any plugins. The trade-off is that not all web browsers display rich HTML5 content (although the volume is increasing), so you may wish to offer special HTML5 services that compliment your mainstream offering.

HTML5 and apps are not necessarily an either/or issue. Because HTML5 offers free access, certain rich features can be available to everyone with an HTML5-compliant browser. The effect on considering apps is to then think about how an app can generate specific revenue for a specific purpose. Can you build a game around your content, for example, which you can then sell through an app store?

PugPig

Pug Pig is an open source project that uses native source code and HTML5 to enable producers to publish interactive books to the iOS, Android. They have created a template - a structure to place your content in - which is available for free to run on OSX. They have also released the source code on GitHub. Pug Pig have taken an efficient and smart approach to App making by using HTML5, so that you can use your existing skills and also re-purpose existing web content in your Apps. This contrasts with the present App authoring convention, which has been for expensive, custom coded productions that don't sit within any sensible workflow - no matter what your budget is. Pug Pig also have a responsive development team that are available online and take part in a wide number of development events and user group meetings.

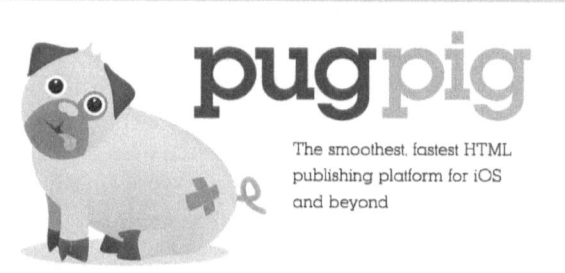

http://pugpig.com/

Xcode template
http://pugpig.com/downloads/PugpigTemplate.pkg

Source code
https://github.com/kaldor/pugpig

Example App
http://itunes.apple.com/us/app/pugpig-guide/id441715052?mt=8&ls=1

Print On Demand (POD), including short run printing

Digital technologies make the process of print publishing much more reactive. With print-on-demand (POD), it is possible to make exactly the right number of books that you need, and to manage your costs more effectively. Gone are the days of bulky minimum orders. Now you can publish a very small number of books, and it's as easy as sending a document to a printer.

POD is a process in which new copies of a document – such as a book – are not printed until an order has been received. POD and short-run press allow for the quantity of a print run to be determined by the author (or publisher). They have a variety of applications, including:

- Building a commercially viable publication where investment is focused on printing only the amount that is necessary, based on projected sales volumes
- Printing in bundles, and offering the work at different price points in order to attract interested consumers. For example, the first edition might cost £7, the next £8, the next £9 and the regular publication £10
- Global printing and fulfilment – since books are printed around the world your freight costs are greatly reduced, opening up foreign markets
- Making special or first editions available, where particular elements have gone into the manufacture of the book, such as a special type of cover or some other artisanal element

POD is therefore a cost-effective solution to a number of issues brought about by volume publishing, and its costs are competitive. A quote for a PDF file consisting of 108 pages, with a height of 229 mm, and a width 152 mm, was £380 to set up, and worked out to £2.28 per unit. The setup fee included an ISBN number allocation, bibliographic data management, file-checking, and printer liaison. An additional £150 would have given basic EPUB conversion, with the author receiving 80 per cent of the net receipts on sales.

It is worth pointing out that POD does not mean

submitting your work to a dull and unimaginative finish. In fact, POD is perfect for artisanal bookmaking. While POD can handle the printing of your book's pages, you can still take care of the binding and art. This is a great way to make a craft-driven process more cost-effective, and it provides further possibilities for revenue. For example, you could offer 'standard' versions of your printed book for £10 on your website and/or through an online retailer, and sell artisanal versions through eBay to the highest bidder. Such a blend of revenue-generation possibilities is likely to sustain interest in your work through an emphasis on higher-value productions.

Don't Panic: Organise!

Mute magazine, OpenMute's sister project, is an online and print publication dealing with topics in culture and politics that relate to developments on the internet. Mute has long since held a light to the benefits of print-on-demand, having used POD and short-run press technologies to produce its magazines and specially commissioned book titles from 2005 onwards. Don't Panic: Organise! is a collection of articles dealing with issues in and around international education struggles. As the movement seemed to be gathering speed, Mute decided to release the material in print and offer it free to groups who were staging an event or demonstration against the government cuts. The format was easy to assemble (as the articles were already in a PDF format), fast and cheap to print. What was produced was a professional looking pamphlet that enabled the quick distribution of knowledge.

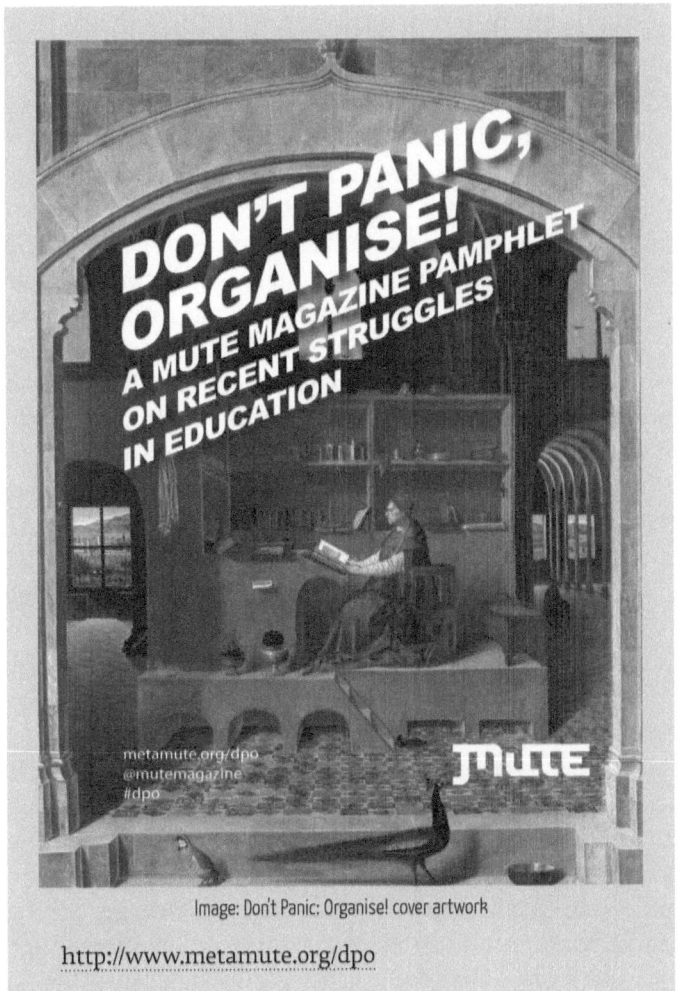

Image: Don't Panic: Organise! cover artwork

http://www.metamute.org/dpo

Some more practical considerations

Making choices in digital publishing requires a great deal of thought and clarity as regards what a publisher or author might ultimately want. From a commercial perspective, one of the most important considerations is the trade-off between reach and revenue. In terms of books, while selling through major retailers such as Amazon or Apple grants the availability and reach producers might desire, these retailers are likely to take a significant cut of revenues – somewhere between 22 and 60 per cent for POD, 30 and 60 per cent for e-books, and around 30 per cent for apps. So, if your chosen route is to sell through the major retailers, then keep your costs low, and don't expect to turn a massive profit overnight.

Alternatively, you could decide to sell your own digital content. Many website content management systems (CMSs) offer 'shopping cart' functionality – the ability to hold a product in the system, and for the customer to pay for it through a well-known service such as PayPal. Here, the customer would visit the 'online store' of your website, select their 'product', pay for it, and then either download it as a file (typically PDF or EPUB) or wait for their POD book to arrive in the post. However, while in this instance you get to keep all of the revenue, the downside is that making your content available across a range of devices will be harder work, and you will need to do your own marketing.

Having said that, the greater reach enabled by using an online retailer will not necessarily increase your audience size either. Publishing work exclusively in digital form increases the onus on a producer to devise a strategy of audience awareness. This could be through your website and associated online presence (Twitter, Facebook, email newsletters, etc.), or various news media, such as arts publications. As a marketing strategy, it is also not uncommon for authors/publishers to make some of their content available for free. For example, a poet may wish to give away a handful of his or her poems online, in the hope of persuading the audience to buy the complete book from Amazon or Apple.

O/R Books

O/R Books offers a compelling example of how to dodge multiple problematic distribution channels. Bucking the trend of disintermediation, O/R opts to be both publisher *and* distributor, luring custom away from the likes of Amazon and other dominant intermediaries, whose inexhaustible drive to consolidate direct relationships with expanding customer bases has permanently altered the book selling business. O/R restrict the distribution of print copies, only allowing direct purchase of their books through their site, ignoring the big players both on and offline by making available only a modest list of titles to retailers/bookshops. This practice allows a higher percentage of profits to go straight to the publisher and author, a well as setting O/R's prices at very reasonable levels (and thus perhaps driving sales that way too).

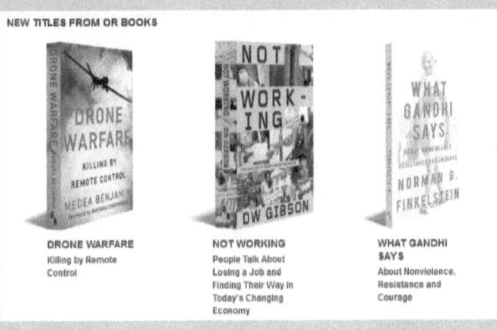

> O/R Books also produce all their titles using POD technology, avoiding the wastage incurred in traditional printing processes. Printing 'as and when needed' also cuts the costs of producing a new title, and spreads it out over the course of its retail lifespan. Overall, it increases the publisher's flexibility, speeding up the whole publishing process so that the physical object can be brought out with relative ease. O/R Books' founders are at pains to emphasise that, due to spending less on printing and distribution, they can dedicate more funds to advertising and marketing, developing creative ways to promote and circulate their books through social media and supplementary content such as video.
>
> http://www.orbooks.com/ & http://vimeo.com/orbooks

Copyright

Considering the actual content itself, it is important to be aware of issues relating to Intellectual Property (IP). This holds as true for newly authored, original material, as it does for the existing material of others (such as a written poem or composed music). With your own material, you should ensure that you incorporate an attribution notice – meaning copyright, copyleft or a legend detailing your own terms of use. This might mean a legend to negate copyright and place your material in the public domain, but it could also function to request acknowledgement by others. Do this somewhere within the work (at the front of the e-book, for example). When you are using material from others, you must ensure that permission has been given to republish it, and that an appropriate citation is made to the work and the publisher. Likewise, if your content is being used elsewhere, even by non-profit organisations, make sure that you are given an acknowledgement.

IP frameworks exist to make these processes easier, but can come with compromises attached. Creative Commons (CC) for example is a global legal framework which is designed to enable a freer exchange of content. The framework has a number of parameters, including NC (Can only be used non-commercially) and ND (Can only be copied and republished in its original form). You may wish to enable Creative Commons licencing on your own work, whichever way you intend to make it available. The benefit of CC is its universal recognition; its compromises are more subtle and therefore difficult to identify. Firstly, CC doesn't address how value is created on the net – in that your non-commercial content still adds value to internet giants to which it will be connected (like Google and Facebook). Secondly, CC doesn't engage with the secondary purpose of IP frameworks, which is to benefit second level businesses specifically designed to exploit copyright and not the authors or creators. To consider these pros and cons and for further information on CC, visit http://www.creativecommons.org.uk

Other copyleft licences, like the GNU Free Documentation Licence, make provisions that any derivative works are also made under a compliant licence. Like with the CC licence, the objective is to ensure a free flow of information and knowledge. See: http://www.gnu.org/copyleft/fdl.html

The GNU Free Documention and Creative Commons licences are both based in a US framework of constitutional rights and the freedom of speech. Additionally however, they are based in US endorsed conceptions of property and commerce – both of which encourage the free flow of ideas, while enshrining strong authorship principles.

Anti-copyright is the third school of IP. In using a variety of agreements to make arrangements for attribution, remuneration and exchange, but refusing relationships based on property, it rejects the current regime. Whereas Copyleft may seek to enshrine freedom through licences, Anti-copyright rejects the existing framework altogether, looking rather for formations which prioritise social justice over property.

Since the law has it that copyright can't actually be given up or disowned by an author, no matter how much s/he would like to, Anti-copyright artists tend to use licences to express their position. The US folk singer and song writer, Woody Guthrie, presents a unique early example in his recordings of the 1940s, which included the following 'Copyright Warning':

> This song is Copyrighted in U.S., under Seal of Copyright # 154085, for a period of 28 years, and anybody caught singin it without our permission, will be mighty good friends of ourn, cause we don't give a dern. Publish it. Write it. Sing it. Swing to it. Yodel it. We wrote it, that's all we wanted to do.

Sound artist, Mattin, also explores ideas around copyright in his contribution to the book, Noise and Capitalism. See: 'Anti-Copyright: why improvisation and noise run against the idea of intellectual property' http://www.arteleku.net/noise_capitalism/

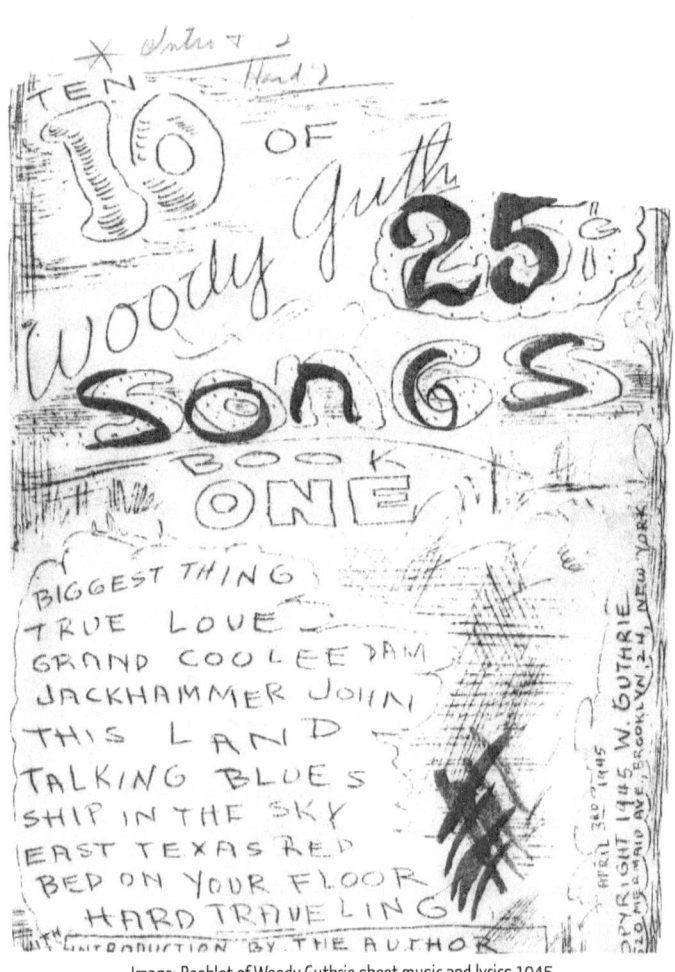

Image: Booklet of Woody Guthrie sheet music and lyrics 1945
See full image set on WikiPedia http://linkme2.net/rn

The future

Digital editorial content has grown up. Where it historically augmented print content in a supporting role – such as with Desktop Publishing – it now occupies a more primary position, being consumed in a bewildering array of spaces and ways and becoming enmeshed in people's daily lives. It is nonetheless worth bearing in mind that, from a consumer and producer's perspective, the availability of mass digital content is only a recent phenomenon, and that many additional forms and use cases will emerge in the years to come. It is highly probable, too, that these will permeate other domestic devices, for example the television.

These changes present opportunities for cultural organisations, even if they complicate the 'digital jungle' further. Digital media strategists often say, 'fish where the fish are' – that is, develop products that your target audience can access easily, using tools that they are already familiar with. The mass reach won by social media tools and popular online retailers makes this easier than ever, although it intensifies the imperative to stand out among the crowd. It is important to remember that digital publishing strategies cannot be separated from digital strategies generally, which in turn cannot be separated from overall cultural or business strategies. For example, if an element of your organisation's business strategy is to increase audience participation, then your digital and digital publishing strategy should reflect that.

Finally, it is important to spot the right trends when assessing exactly how publishing can play a role in your work. Ask your existing customers how they want to access your content in the future (an overlooked and often important point), look at what other arts organisations and producers are doing and, above all, don't be afraid to experiment.

2
Video
A new era of public service publishing?

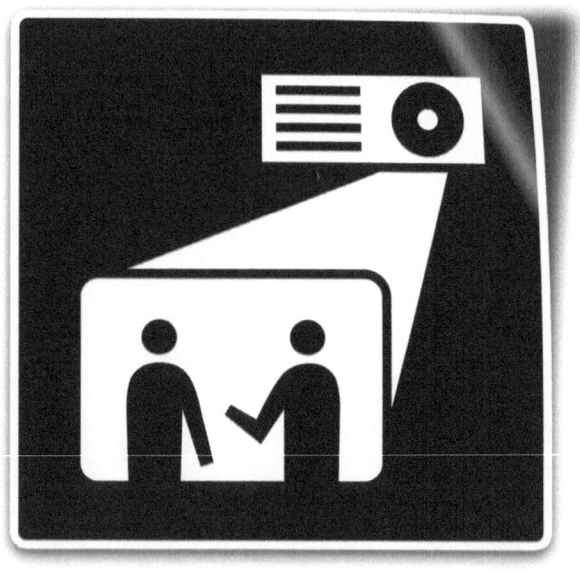

Recent years have seen a dramatic growth in the amount of video content available on the internet, for which there are two main technical reasons: the ever greater penetration of broadband and the massive advances in the technology available both to generate and consume video across networks. It is now possible to view good-quality internet video not just on computers, but on mobiles, tablets and on television. Smartphones, particularly those using the latest iOS (iPhone) and Android operating systems, can play short videos in very high quality, while an increasing number of devices have sockets so they can play their video content on an HD TV. 'Smart TVs' are starting to enter the market, which feature services to view online video, while other devices, such as DVD players and games consoles, are also starting to feature such functionality.

There is now a much greater flexibility in distribution too. Until very recently, watching video productions was an act effectively controlled by state broadcasters (in television), or by tightly-controlled distributors (in cinema and home video). These frameworks have been fundamentally disrupted, and there are now far fewer barriers in the way of making work available to a global audience. You can choose to offer your content across a multitude of different video publishing services, as well as exhibit locally without going to a cinema. Galleries, halls, and public spaces often have projection facilities for computers, where film-makers can present their latest work.

Cameras, filming and post-production

Modern digital cameras – those from the last five years – are usually able to connect direct to a computer, so that the material can be downloaded straight from the camera to the computer's hard disk. This can be done irrespective of whether the camera uses tape, DVD, or its own hard disk to record. However, such domestic cameras, such as the popular Flip range by Cisco, often have limited value. They store a limited amount of footage, come with poor sound quality, and provide limited HD size and resolution (enough for 'rough' use, but not for a polished production). Although more expensive to buy, a good-quality HD camera will provide much higher visual quality.

Of course, it's possible to use any camera for online video. It's really up to you as to how you want to offer your work. The introduction of the webcam, for example, has democratised video production down to the individual user at no cost. Most middle-range laptops now come complete with an integrated webcam, primarily intended for video calling use (such as Skype).

Webcams and network cameras offer a tremendous possibility for artists working with physical matter. Where an installation or artwork changes its physicality, watching it change through a webcam can be of interest to audiences. Artists who want to provide this feature should ask their host organisation to examine the possibility of a live feed to accompany their work. Similarly, helmetcams – small video cameras and recorders attached to helmets – provide greater scope for mobile filming, although for outdoor filming some additional equipment may be required.

One & Other

One & Other was Antony Gormley's project to occupy the vacant space of the fourth plinth in Trafalgar Square, between July and October 2009. The work was shown live on the internet, with a fixed webcam capturing every moment of the plinth's occupation.

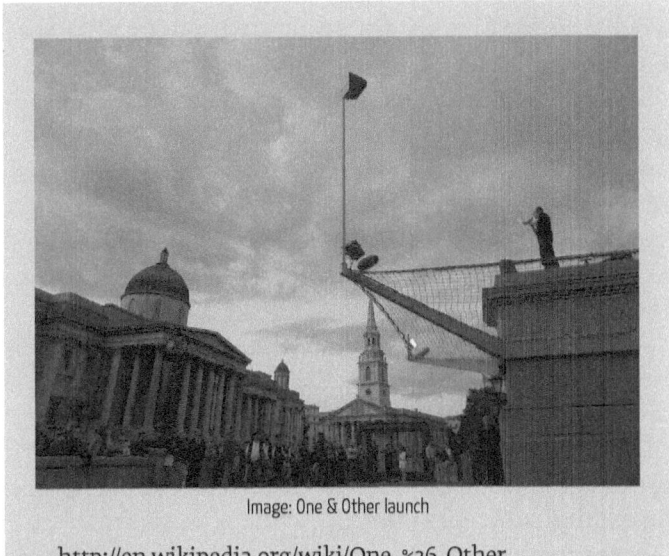
Image: One & Other launch
http://en.wikipedia.org/wiki/One_%26_Other

For filming in buildings, although it may be easy to set up and operate equipment, for optimum quality there are a number of issues to consider. The first is the size and shape of the space. Filming in small rooms can often deliver poor visual and acoustic results, as the camera attempts to fit in too much. Larger areas are better as they offer more scope for pan and zoom, and wherever possible an external microphone should be used, enabling directional recording to provide a greater quality of audio, particularly in speech. Likewise, a standing tripod, as opposed to the smaller, table-mounted tripod, will cut down on wobble caused by floor vibration.

Having captured your footage, online video increases the options available for editing and post-production. The 'traditional' means of making a video, where raw footage is physically sent to an edit suite, is becoming increasingly irrelevant for many, particularly those who are looking to make and distribute video content with a small budget. Editing and post-production treatment is now commonly undertaken entirely within software, and many good-quality editing tools are available for free. As the web becomes increasingly capable of offering interactivity, some websites now offer video editing tools directly within the browser. However, the quality of these will vary, and the range of functions will be less than is offered with an installed software package.

If you don't want to edit your work yourself, it is possible to farm it out to post-production specialists, who can bid for the work. They receive the raw footage and return the film complete. However, as with all situations where you are handing work to a third party, exercise caution, asking for examples and references.

Yet another option would be to blow the process wide open. Some film-makers and producers of online video are publishing their raw footage directly to the web, asking viewers to edit and republish it themselves, sometimes as part of a competition. As well as inviting active participation, this also helps to spread awareness of the work.

Content

With the increased ease of video production comes the opportunity to provide an ever wider array of content. For example, it is much easier now to make old material available digitally. Recordings made on VHS, Beta, Super 8, DV / MiniDV and so on can be digitised by professional conversion companies. Many well-known chains of photographic retailers will provide this service, and other businesses provide it by mail order. Whatever your choice, please ask the vendor about their approach to quality – in most cases, you will want an exact replica of the originating tape, without degradation of audio or video quality. If possible, send high quality duplicates if you are working with a mail order vendor, and retain the original tapes for yourself, securely stored off-site.

Deptford.TV

Deptford.TV is an audio-visual documentation of urban change in Deptford. The Deptford.TV website contains a full archive of the captured material, spanning several years, as well as a guide on how to make and distribute your own video material online, with the use of free and open source software.

Image: DepfordTV diaries book –
http://metamute.org/services/openmute-press/deptford.tv-diaries

http://watch.deptford.tv/blog/

Of course, online video can play a major role in showcasing performances to audiences. Recorded video material, made available after the event, will build the level of interest and engagement with the work, the performers, and the setting. Also, small clips of a performance before the first night – such as in rehearsal – are often useful to audiences, who will be able to get a clearer idea of what to expect when seeing the performance in actuality.

> ### Sadler's Wells
>
> The international dance venue in the heart of London has a selection of over 200 performances. They have been published to YouTube and then incorporated throughout the organisation's own website, for maximum coverage and relevance.
>
> http://www.youtube.com/user/sadlerswells

It may also be possible to offer 'behind the scenes' footage, including videos of rehearsals or other preparation, which give viewers the chance to learn more about work being performed whilst also providing an opportunity to become acquainted with those working in the background of a project – the technicians, producers, and other associated members. Such video could include interviews with specific individuals, and, to make the whole process even more interactive, viewers could be asked to submit their own questions.

Philharmonia Orchestra

A resident of the Southbank Centre, the Orchestra's web offering features a comprehensive set of 'behind the scenes' interviews with conductors and performers. It's a great way to get to know more about the performance – both before and after the 'main event'.

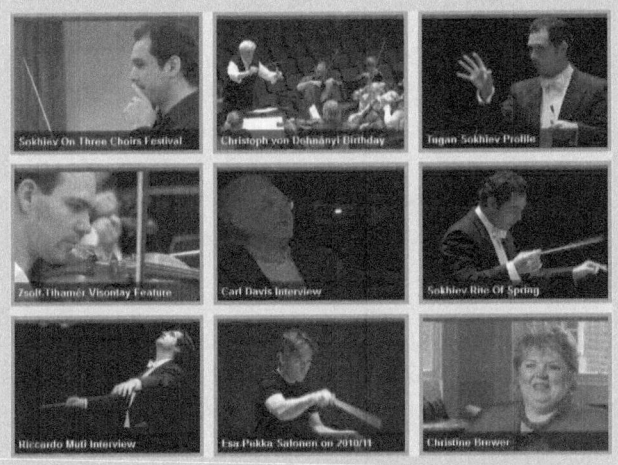
Image: screengrab from website

http://www.philharmonia.co.uk/thesoundexchange/backstage/interviews/

There is also the possibility of live coverage. This is a development that, until recently, would have been practically impossible for anyone to offer, except for the major broadcasters, however live broadcast is now increasingly available as a low-cost option, with free publishers starting to offer it too. Ustream is the most popular service, although YouTube is expected to offer a similar service very soon. This is likely to be an option for one-off events, or performances with significant interest which take place at smaller or hard-to-reach venues.

Live video works through the near-instantaneous encoding of digital video from the camera, and the live upload of the encoded data to a server. The server then 'pushes' the data directly to the internet through an online video player. From the perspective of the viewer, since the content is made available through a browser, this means that additional plug-ins are not generally required. However, in some cases, external software will be necessary, depending on the format and type of the broadcast, for example if it is part of a Skype/VOIP video conference. It is important to let your audience know what is required before broadcasting.

Offering live video requires a robust internet connection with a good upload speed, tested before live broadcast commences. Ensure that the broadband connection to be used is capable of handling a live broadcast for your intended duration, and contact your Internet Service Provider (ISP) if you want to be sure. The more you have used the equipment before in any capacity, the more confident you can be of a good outcome.

You will also need a computer with a good specification to handle the capture and live-encoding of data. Cheaper netbooks and laptops are not recommended for live broadcasts at a good size and/or resolution (HD quality in particular). A high quality laptop or desktop computer is recommended, as well as the latest versions of any of the three popular operating systems (Windows, Mac, Linux).

Many live streams suffer from poor production qualities, even when the bandwidth is fine. This is because the camera is often positioned in a static space, using the integrated microphone, to capture people moving around a wide space. So, in addition to thorough testing, ensuring good bandwidth and a good computer, you should also have someone in charge of the camera and equipment.

They will need to take charge, monitoring the quality of the broadcast for the duration of the event. This is where social media services can really play to your advantage as you can encourage commentary. Twitter is a particularly good tool for canvassing live opinion. If someone tweets that the audio is too quiet, there will need to be someone on hand to do something about it.

Finally, to ensure you have a polished production of the broadcast available online afterwards, have someone on hand with a professional-grade audio recorder to capture it in high quality, which can then be subject to editing and post-production.

Distribution

With the proliferation of wireless broadband and the increasing availability of cheap laptops, bandwidth has grown considerably over the years, making it easier than ever to upload video from practically anywhere (although being so mobile inevitably has an implication on cost). But to get the most out of the technology available there are a few factors worth bearing in mind.

Bandwidth, meaning the speed at which data is transferred over a connection, is most commonly measured in Megabits per second (Mbps). Broadband connections in many premises (including homes) are between 0.5 and 2mbps, with the latter being the speed that the UK Government wants all broadband connections to reach by 2015. According to ThinkBroadband, a 200MB file – around 45 minutes of video – would take 15 minutes to upload at 2Mbps. However, this speed can be greatly affected by, for example, the distance from your premises to the telephone exchange, the contention ratio (i.e. how many other people are connected to your line, and whether they are using it at the same time), and the age of the equipment that your Internet Service Provider is using to connect you.

It is also worth pointing out here that most broadband connections are asynchronous. This means that the speed of sending data (uploading) is not as fast as receiving data (downloading). It is often around half the speed. This is something to keep in mind if you're expecting to be making a lot of video material and sending a lot of data to online servers.

While producers of online video would traditionally have offered their work as a file to download – typically in Quicktime, MPEG or Windows Video (WMV) format – video is now most commonly viewed by streaming data directly through a browser, using, for the most part, a Flash-based video player. Flash is a multimedia technology, with the player embedded into most web browsers. This is how popular public video publishing services such as YouTube, Vimeo, and DailyMotion offer their content. Viewing on a mobile device often takes place through specific apps which provide a similar service. The more common video services offer streaming through a vast array of servers, meaning that video can be watched by a large number of users simultaneously.

With video publishing services, there are dedicated programs available to upload content. This allows you to upload your work without requiring the web browser to be open. However, uploading video of any duration and file size will require a broadband connection which is constantly available. Ideally, you will want to use a computer which has a wired connection to your broadband modem, although if you have a robust, reliable wireless network within your building, then this should also work. The probability of a successful upload decreases when using public and mobile wireless. Here, upload speed can be slow and also prone to 'drops', although it is more reliable in areas with strong coverage, such as cities and large towns.

There are many different options available for presenting your content to an audience. Creating a channel on a public video publishing service, such as YouTube, is a popular way of making content easily and widely available and means you can consolidate your video material into one place. All you have to do is communicate the URL (web address) of your channel. Many organisations offer a link from their website to their video channel page. Alternatively, public publishing services will allow you to embed your videos within your own website once they've been published (most services will offer you a chunk of code to do so).

That said, offering video content does not necessarily mean signing up to one of the larger publishing services if you don't want to. Many web hosting companies and Internet Service Providers offer streaming services, providing tools of a similar nature.

> ### Tate Channel
>
> The Tate has developed its own catalogue of self-produced videos, detailing exhibitions and talks at the gallery, along with coverage of important events around the world such as the Venice Biennale.
>
> http://channel.tate.org.uk/

You do not necessarily have to publish your content for all to see either. Some services allow you to limit the distribution of your content. If you are offering 'premium content' – such as a live or on-demand performance in full length – then this could be available behind a login, where viewers would have to register. In doing so, you have the possibility of capturing the email addresses of your audience, which can then be used for marketing purposes – such as announcing future performances or special offers.

Also, because online video allows you to publish many times, you can try out content on your audience, even before it is released for wider distribution. For example, you could publish a work-in-progress video to a password-protected space on your website, giving the password to selected contacts. Inviting feedback could play a crucial role in the development of your work.

Another option would be to publish to a Facebook wall, perhaps offering small clips and inviting your audience to view longer length material elsewhere. Facebook Video allows for the publishing of video directly to Facebook, with the advantage of offering the content to an audience that is already engaged – either as a fan or as a friend, depending on how your content is made available.

Institute of Contemporary Arts

The ICA runs a busy Facebook page full of news, coverage, and live streaming of its talks and other events, using the Livestream app.

https://www.facebook.com/icalondon

You might also consider distributing through a P2P (peer-to-peer) network such as BitTorrent. Rather than downloading from a central location, P2P works by gathering up the constituent parts of a file from a range of users, then 'spreading' the download between them. The more people that have parts of the file, the faster the download. P2P networks have often been seen as sources of piracy, because they offer easy ways to upload and download large files between many people, however they are becoming increasingly valuable as a legitimate and highly effective means of distribution, particularly for longer pieces of work.

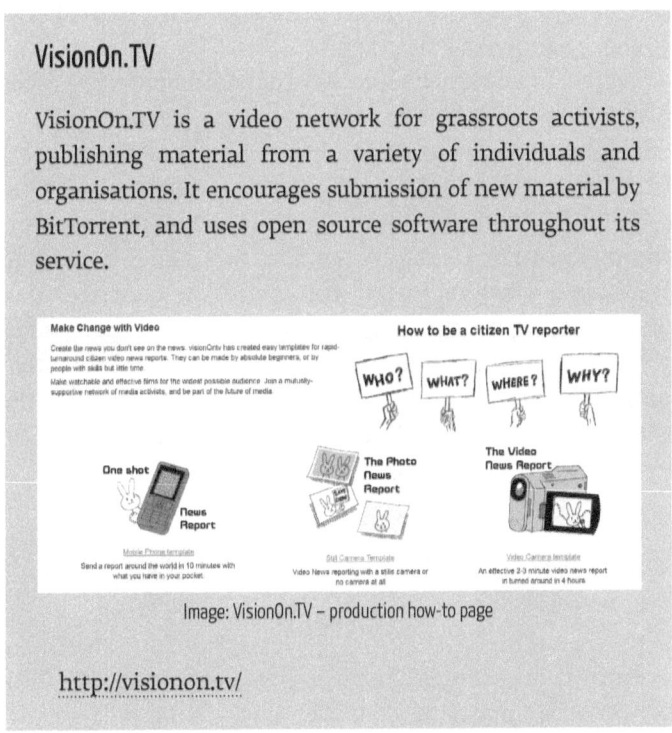

VisionOn.TV

VisionOn.TV is a video network for grassroots activists, publishing material from a variety of individuals and organisations. It encourages submission of new material by BitTorrent, and uses open source software throughout its service.

Image: VisionOn.TV – production how-to page

http://visionon.tv/

Although, as mentioned, Adobe Flash is currently the most popular tool for watching video content through a web browser, this is about to change with the advent of HTML5. HTML5 is the next version of HTML, the mark-up language that is at the core of every single web page. With HTML5, video plays directly through the browser, so there is no need for a Flash player to load first. HTML5 is starting to be offered as an option by the larger video publishing services including YouTube and Vimeo. Mobile users are currently the biggest recipients of HTML5 availability. To make the most of this, your website, or at least the pages that play video, will need to be HTML5-compliant. There are many free tools available for web developers to do this, and it will make your work much more appealing, particularly to those using a mobile phone.

As outlined earlier, an increasing number of televisions under the 'Smart TV' umbrella term are becoming IPTV-enabled, as are consumer gaming devices such as the Xbox from Microsoft, and Sony's Playstation 3. Because of IPTV's relationship with television – particularly HD – it offers the opportunity to display visually rich work. Accessing IPTV-ready content is not too dissimilar from general web browsing from a computer. IPTV devices usually offer some form of basic web browser, although they are often proprietary browsers that interpret web pages (particularly the more complex ones) in different ways. As for the video itself, most devices will play them in a variety of formats.

A word about selling and marketing your content

Online video content can easily become part of a commercial model. It does not have to be free. Many e-commerce systems cater for the payment of intangible goods, such as software or books. Such systems, many of which are free and easy to integrate, can also cater for video – either as downloadable files, or to allow the right to view a video on a particular page (pay-per-view). You may also wish to offer special passes to view or download a whole set of works – such as ten films, or 50 views. Again, many e-commerce services can provide such a facility. Paying can be undertaken by a payment intermediary such as PayPal.

MUBI Europe

Film platform, MUBI, provides a rare example of a mature art film platform whose users are willing to pay for content. Films are sold as quality streams to be watched on your computer, ranging from £0.69 for a single film to a flat, monthly watch-all-you-want price of around £6.29. The videos come from small to mainstream distributors – the most interesting part of the service being the way it allows for the editorialising and community sorting of material. For example, you might find a list of women directors compiled by a user and use this to browse further content.

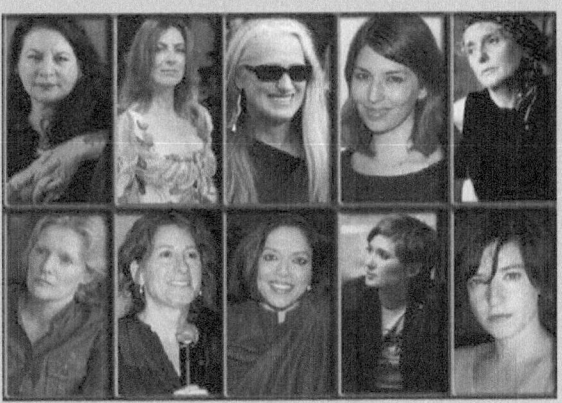

Image: Women directors page graphic

http://mubi.com

Women directors listing:
http://mubi.com/lists/female-directors-on-ubuweb

Marketing your video starts with having good metadata. Metadata are the labels that describe your work. They are like the DNA that runs throughout online content in all its different shapes and sizes. If a viewer is presented with a single search box, then they expect the search function to return accurate, high quality results. The greater the metadata, the more chance your audience will have of finding the right video at the first attempt. For a video clip, such labels might include: the name of the work; the genre; the location; people within the work; the date of production; the copyright holder; the price; whether the video is in colour or monochrome; and a short sentence describing the work. This will ensure that your video is easier to discover across different search engines, particularly if you are publishing to a public video publishing service.

3
Archiving

Avoiding digital dodos, keeping your work in circulation

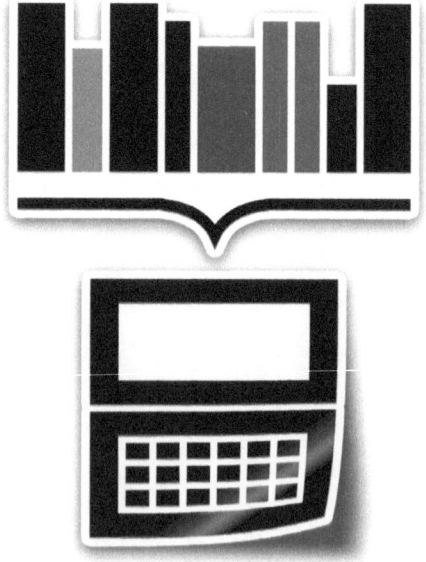

Options have increased dramatically in recent years for large-scale digital archiving. Until very recently, the archiving of digital material involved recording onto hard media, such as a DVD or tape, which in turn had to be stored in a physical location. Nowadays, increasing internet bandwidth has led to a growth in companies offering 'cloud' storage space on servers connected to the internet, so that files of any sort can be automatically archived direct from a computer, whilst for projects that require a more sophisticated approach there is the possibility of setting up an online database at relatively little cost.

As well as being cheaper than their physical alternative, digital archives are also very easy to maintain and manage. Like all data on the internet, they are flexible and can be managed according to the needs of the individual owner. Archiving can be performed by one person or collaboratively across a dispersed group of people and it's possible to quickly change the configuration of archives' management, hosting and delivery, as well as the quality and depth of information within them. With the right know-how, archives in digital form are also much easier to index, which helps facilitate rapid retrieval and access. By offering an archive online, you are presenting work in a way that is quick for audiences to access and use. They can be entirely open-access, or they can be password-protected.

However, despite these advantages, there are some important issues to consider before building your own archive, particularly if you intend on storing data with a third party on commercial terms. Firstly, it is important to think carefully about who you are entrusting your data to. You should ask them about their data management processes and procedures and check their terms and conditions thoroughly. Also, you must be aware of the implications surrounding copyright. Before signing any contract, you should ensure that you are not surrendering any rights to your material. Archiving is inextricably linked with intellectual property. Indeed, many artists enjoy a stream of income which lasts many years, if not decades, from their archived work. Yet, others believe creative production comes from, and should move freely back into, a generalised human creativity – where copyright should hold no sway whatsoever. In light of these different approaches, we encourage artists and organisations to approach copyright in a way that reflects their working ethos. Consider your position in relation to the twin imperatives of access and remuneration, while not allowing things to become overly complex or restrictive. Creative Commons offers a useful model for consideration; it allows for an intellectual property model to be placed onto an archive in its entirety, whilst making the access and usage rights abundantly clear.

In some cases, such as with commercial art galleries, archives can be offered under subscription models and these are fairly straightforward to manage. Organisations can take payment through PayPal, WorldPay or another widely-used service and the customer can have access for a specified period. Some archive systems will take care of this automatically, while others offer very simple account management tools, in which case it is the responsibility of the account manager to expire accounts when they have reached the end of their subscription period. In both cases, customers should be given prior notice of their subscription expiry, alongside the opportunity to extend their subscription if necessary.

Developing a digital archive

If your digital presence is something worth preserving, as it should be, then digital archiving makes sense. However, it requires a considered strategy that addresses what is to be archived, how it is to be archived, the extent of the archive, and how much it will cost. Digital archiving is an investment, and a good strategy will mean that this investment benefits both yourself and your potential audience for years to come.

If you work for an organisation and are considering a web-based archive, then you may wish to offer access to a select number of people. In most cases, this is easy to do, and is not too dissimilar to how a content management system (CMS) manages website content. Where your archive has many authors, ensure that there is an audit trail, so you can see what has been input, when, and by whom. The audit trail doesn't have to be visible to all, but it exists as a part of the archive management process.

National Portfolio Organisation archives

Many National Portfolio Organisation's have records of their work on their websites. Some have digitized their actual works to make available either for free or to sell. However, there are not many that have large database-sized archives. Here are some examples of NPO's that have done particularly effective or interesting archiving.

- Art Monthly - magazine with archive of past issues available to subscribers or to buy as individual issues. http://www.artmonthly.co.uk/magazine/site/search
- Whitechapel Gallery Archive – extensive online

> archive of various works produced by the gallery.
> http://archive.whitechapelgallery.org/
> - Institute of Contemporary Arts – small archive of talks available freely.
>   http://www.ica.org.uk/archive
> - Lux – digital archive of film and video, a small part of physical archive, available to view for free.
>   http://lux.org.uk/collection/videos
> - Siobhan Davies Relay – archives of talks from past events freely available.
>   http://www.siobhandavies.com/conversations/

Cloud storage

Many cloud storage services are offered for free by software vendors as part of the operating system. This is the case with Ubuntu One, a cloud storage system that comes as part of the Ubuntu operating system. 2GB is offered for free, with the option to extend this without any disruption to the files themselves. Files to be synchronised to the cloud are placed in an Ubuntu One folder on the computer and this folder tends to become the location for documents for many users, as all files are then automatically synchronised. The files can be accessed and retrieved through a web browser, if, for example, the computer on which the original material is saved cannot be accessed. A Windows client is shortly to become available for Ubuntu One, making access to Ubuntu's cloud even easier, whilst Apple's iCloud provides a similar service for the Mac.

Another example that is currently in development is Syncany, a cross-platform, open-source file sharing application. Unlike the other solutions, with Syncany you remain in control of where your files are published. For example, they could be stored in an FTP or Secure FTP server, or Amazon's S3 cloud storage for example. It also secures the local copies of the sychronised files (i.e. those on the computer).

Dropbox is another option, and at a more advanced stage than Syncany. This is a popular solution as storage can be increased easily and there are phone apps which increase the options for viewing and controlling your cloud-based files.

Databases

Databases are, of course, one of the most common and traditional ways to store structured information and the web is well-suited to the display of, and interaction with, large-scale databases. Indeed, many websites are effectively driven by databases. Historically, databases have been commercial, proprietary, and run on local computers. However, this changed with the advent of MySQL, which has become one of the world's most popular database systems.

MySQL runs on a web server and is commonly accessed through a web browser. You don't need anything connected to the internet in order to run such a service; you can run a popular collection of applications on a standalone computer. The most well-known suite of products is LAMP, standing for Linux (operating system), Apache (web server), MySQL (database) and PHP (programming language). Ubuntu has a quick-start page on how to install the LAMP suite. Versions of this suite exist for other operating systems, such as MAMP (Mac) and WAMP (Windows).

Getting started with MySQL is fairly easy to do. You can

set up a database in minutes, and quickly develop some code in PHP to output the results from the database, as well as provide a web page to input the data if many people are inputting from a variety of locations – which may be the case if you have a large archive and want it to be co-operatively developed. PHPMyAdmin can perform this task, but is ideally for administrative use only, and not for general access.

If a web interface is not what you need right now, then you can also access the MySQL database through local software, called MySQL GUI tools (GUI stands for graphical user interface). They are available to download for free for Windows, Mac, and Linux.

Because MySQL is open source, many other front-end packages are also available, such as HeidiSQL for Windows, and Sequel Pro for Mac OS, which also import spreadsheet files and convert them into databases.

> Install the LAMP suite
> https://help.ubuntu.com/community/ApacheMySQLPHP
>
> PHPMyAdmin
> http://www.phpmyadmin.net/home_page/
>
> MySQL GUI tools
> http://dev.mysql.com/downloads/gui-tools/5.0.html
>
> HeidiSQL
> http://www.heidisql.com/
>
> Sequel Pro
> http://www.sequelpro.com/

Adding content

Obviously, the precise nature of your archive, its design and functionality, will depend on what is to be archived and how it is to be used, but in any case one of the most important things to make sure of when you add content is that it remains readily accessible. In order for your archive to be easily searchable, it is important to adequately describe each component as it is added. Increasingly important to information management and retrieval is the ability to manage and develop metadata – literally, data about data. Metadata is one of the driving forces in terms of how information is offered and found on the internet. The key to providing good metadata is detail and consistency. It's a good idea to create metadata for as many items to be archived as possible so that the person or people managing the archive can ensure that it contains all the relevant materials and users of the archive can find what they're looking for quickly and easily.

It's also a good idea to take a step back before adding material to your archive and to gather up all of the output to be considered and look at it from the perspective of data. This will enable you to create a structure, or schema, that describes what your archive as a whole is about as well as the fields within it. One of the main methods for developing this schema is through the Resource Description Framework (RDF). RDF is used in websites around the world, where interrogation and retrieval are critical, providing consistency as to how data is described. Many large organisations use RDF to index their archives and collections. The British Library offers its entire dataset in RDF, and has licenced it through Creative Commons.

By using the RDF model, you end up with a document containing information about all of the works. You don't necessarily have to worry about writing it all yourself because, like HTML, you can use tools to produce and refine your own RDF. One such tool is Protege, an open source editor which is well-supported and requires Java to run (it can also run natively on Mac OS).

> The British Library offers its entire dataset in RDF
> http://www.bl.uk/bibliographic/datafree.html

> Protege
> http://protege.stanford.edu/

Theatricalia – an audiences' archive

Theatricalia is history being reassembled as audiences and participants piece together a complex mosaic of theatre performances creating a hyperlinked web of plays, performance dates, actors, venues, observations and associated media; flyers and photographs. The site started in 2008 as an experiment to piece together the details of performances based on copies of a few performance programmes and has continued to grows as more people dust off their personal collections and upload them. The site can create an over complex set of connections as you move from a play to an actor and onto a new venue, while skipping through five decades but the model sets out an interesting area to explore.

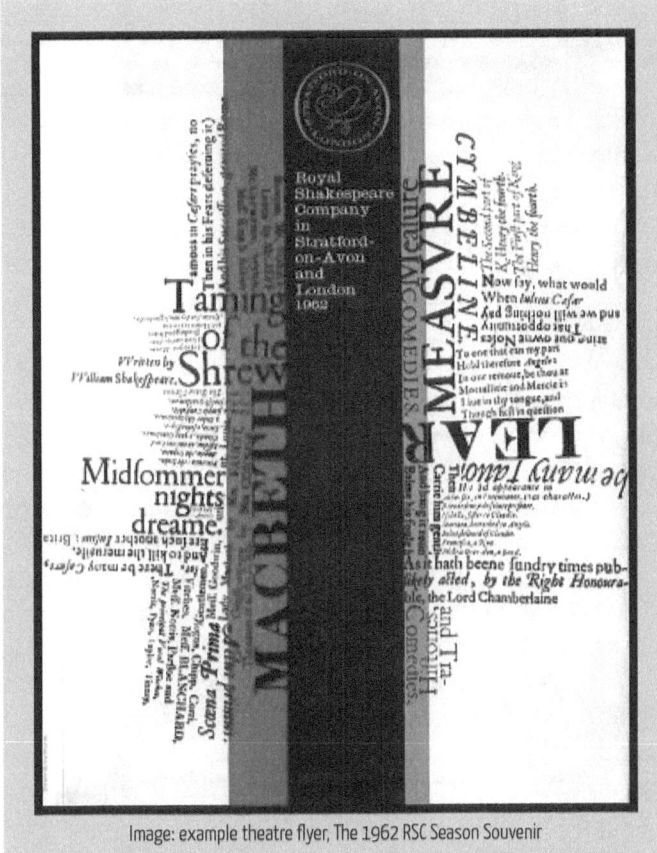

Image: example theatre flyer, The 1962 RSC Season Souvenir

http://theatricalia.com/

Chapter 3: Archiving

Access and Security

Access to your archive does not have to be free and open to all. Many organisations see their archive as a piece of intellectual property that has an intrinsic commercial value, and so want to ensure that they have a degree of control over access. This is often because they do not want copies of the work to be republished on other sites without permission, which, particularly in the case of images, is quite easy to do.

Perhaps the easiest way to restrict access is to have the archive password-protected. It is possible to offer a brief glimpse of the archive – perhaps a web page that describes what it contains – so that users can then request a username and password from the archive owner, who will make the final decision as to who has access and who doesn't. This is effectively offering the archive as an Extranet – a website that is connected to the internet, but is only available to a given proportion of the audience.

When offering access in this way, do ensure that those signing up have agreed to a set of terms and conditions and that these have been checked over by a lawyer. Also, to avoid the possibility of hacking, make sure that the password you provide contains as many variations of upper and lower case letters, numbers and punctuation as possible. This is particularly important for archives which are to be connected to the internet.

Whether your archive is hosted locally (on your computer or the local network) or on the internet (in the cloud or with a web host), you should ensure that you make a regular backup, and that this backup is not stored in the same place as the archive. As an archive grows and becomes increasingly important, the inherent risks increase too. It is vital not to get into a situation where an archive spanning many years is lost forever. You may even wish to consider having you archive insured, given its intellectual and/or commercial value to you and to your audience.

Off-site storage is strongly recommended as an option, irrespective of how your archive is offered. Off-site storage works by taking a copy and having it hosted by a storage company. You will need to work out how to back up your work to disc, which in most cases is not difficult. There are many open source packages that provide DVD authoring, including DVD Flick and DVDStyler. With a database, you will need to back up the SQL file. Do remember to test the copy on disc afterwards. You can then store a copy off-site. Once that is done, consider how frequently you would like to undertake this activity. If you are frequently updating your archive, then storing a DVD copy on a monthly basis may be a good idea. If you are updating less frequently, then every six months may be more appropriate.

As well as CDs and DVDs, you may also consider backing up to a local hard drive, although these can be prone to failure. It would be safer to store a copy of your archive on a local hard drive rather than the main version. Also Flash storage, such as a USB stick, is another option. This is a cheap and easy way to transport files from one place to another. It can be an effective way of running an archive on a local machine; for example, when taking an archive into a school. However, they are easy to lose. Like a hard drive, they should only be used to save copies and to transport data. You should not depend on them as a file store.

4
Open Source
The where, why, what and who!

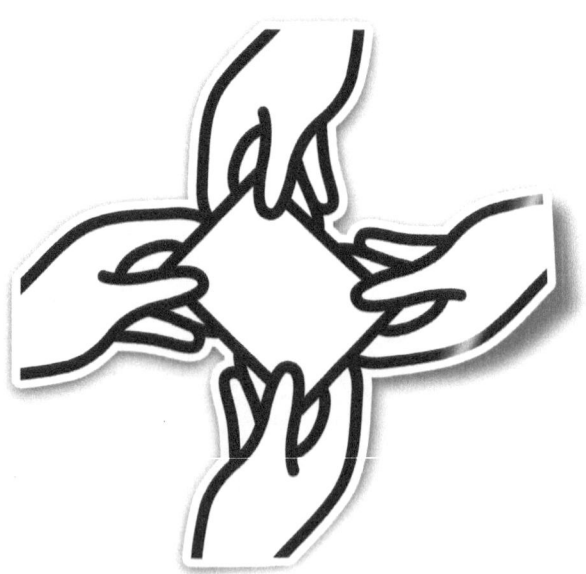

What is open source?

Software is comprised of source code, which is compiled into a working program. Traditionally, people have acquired, installed and run the compiled programs in their finished form. However, a range of technical, social and economic factors – foremost among them a greater, general interconnectivity – have led to a development whereby the source code itself is made available to share, adapt and reuse. This is known as open source. In many cases, pre-compiled versions of the source code are offered as open source software. Most people will not want or need to be aware of the underlying code simply to run the program. However, if they wish to they can make improvements upon the original product or use all or part of the code for entirely different purposes, creating new products, known as 'forks'.

Open source code, software and other materials are usually offered for free: there is no charge to download it, as code or as a compiled program, the particular terms of use being outlined in a licence. There are many freely available options for licencing, from which the originating producer can choose. These are illustrated later in the guide.

Why has open source become popular?

Open source has become popular in software development, as people and organisations can deliver better software with shorter production times. Developers looking to build new software might find that there are some parts already available for what they are trying to do and will therefore not have to spend time on it themselves, particularly if that part has already been developed to a high standard.

Obviously, the major propellant of open source has been the mass adoption of the internet (including, and cutting across, individual, professional, consumer and technical development environments). Before this, it would have been practically impossible to be fully aware of what was being shared and by whom. Now, many repositories exist for hosting and locating open source software, to help you to achieve practically anything, whether you are a software developer or an end-user.

> **Goto10**
>
> Goto10 is an artists and programmers collective working with open source tools and communities. Goto10 have run festivals such as 'Make Art', as well as supporting major software projects such as the PureDyne Linux multimedia operating system. Goto10 have been very active in the PureData community, developing a multimedia performance software suite, also via performances and code contributions.
>
> http://goto10.org/

Has open source been successful?

In some ways, open source has been more successful than commercial software, offering a level of professionalism entirely consistent with commercial packages. The Apache web server, for example, which is free and open source, is the most popular web server in the world. Some of the world's most popular websites, such as Twitter, Wikipedia and Facebook, are built on open source software, with the organisations behind these three services actively giving back to the open source community by offering new software and new code.

Various incarnations of the Unix operating system are free and open source, including Linux, which in itself has various incarnations, called 'distributions', including Ubuntu, Debian, Fedora, and OpenSUSE. These are free to download and retain their commitment to open source. The success of Linux in a commercial capacity is illustrated by the fact that it runs the 10 fastest supercomputers in the world.

Many content management systems for the web are open source, and have powered thousands of sophisticated websites and blogs at a fraction of the cost of commercial content management systems. These include Drupal, Joomla and WordPress, as well as many of their 'plug-ins', which offer additional functionality.

It has also provided alternative day-to-day software packages and suites, including OpenOffice and its related package, LibreOffice. Both of these are full 'office' operating systems, which rival Microsoft Office and are compatible with Microsoft's file formats. Similarly, the open source animation software, Blender, has been used for many short animations, including children's animation, and delivers production quality levels to rival Pixar's.

Many governments have pushed their public agencies to embrace open source. The Brazilian government is one of the world's most active public sector supporters of it, with Linux running across its public agencies and in all state schools. Closer to home, the UK government's Cabinet Office has been active in pushing suppliers to embrace open source, as a way to maximise value in public sector IT spending, which in the UK represents around £20bn per year.

PAD.MA (Public Access Digital Media Archive)

Pad.ma is a free to use, textually annotated, video archive which uses the Open Source video archive framework pan. do/ra. Pad.ma has worked with a variety of international partners on continued development of the video system, with major updates and releases happening in 2012.

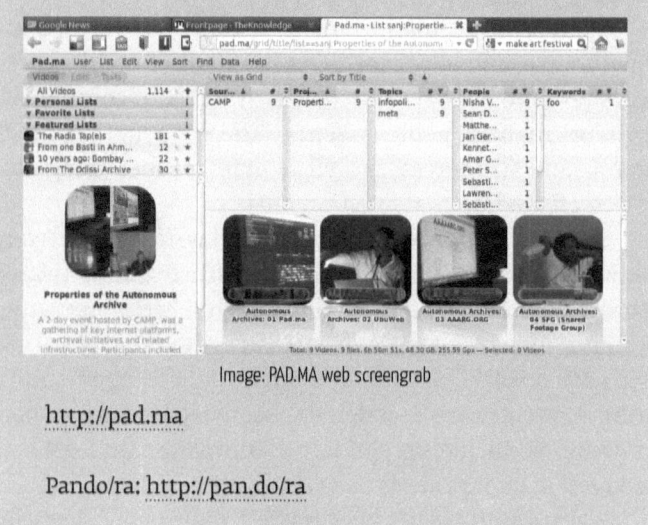

Image: PAD.MA web screengrab

http://pad.ma

Pando/ra: http://pan.do/ra

Finding open source software

Specific search engines and hosts (called 'repositories', 'repos' or 'forges') exist for open source software, so finding it needn't be too strenuous a task. If you are looking to write open source software yourself, then you may find any of the below useful in terms of making your project available to a community of programmers and end-users.

Many news services provide the latest announcements on open source software. FreshMeat is one of the biggest, but is effectively a 'version announcement' system, in that it automatically reports on changes to software rather than publishing stories about their improvements. Something a little easier on the eye is Yahoo's Open Source news service.

Finding open source materials which are not software is harder. There are no repositories, although some types of material, such as text and imagery, can be used on some repositories, such as GitHub. Wikipedia offers some pointers for open source practices elsewhere, such as in film.

SourceForge

SourceForge covers around 300,000 open source projects from around the world. Although the site is free to use, it is actually owned and managed by a private company, GeekNet. It is probably the best known of the open source repositories and is now over a decade old. It provides a hosting environment for open source projects, so that producers can co-develop and publicise their work. There is also a wiki for producers to develop documentation and manuals. SourceForge covers software across all platforms, making it the most likely 'first stop' for Windows users, as well as software developers and those that are interested in the wider open source community.

Launchpad

Launchpad provides a similar set of functions, although is geared towards Linux (the Launchpad service itself is managed by Canonical, the company behind Ubuntu).

Savannah

Savannah again provides similar services, but is younger, smaller, and with a narrower focus. It acts as a central repository for software which is covered under the GNU licence, which we shall discuss later.

Free Software Directory

A collaboration between the Free Software Foundation and Unesco, this is a concise, structured directory of the free software that runs on free operating systems (basically Linux variants). It is quite thin on the ground at the moment. At the time of writing, OpenOffice is listed but not LibreOffice, suggesting that some work is needed to keep it up to date, but it does act as a good starting point if you are keen to use open source software as a consumer and are running, or seeking to run, a variant of Linux.

GitHub

The odd name is down to a system called Git (yes, really) that provides version control for software development. Projects which are hosted on GitHub can be 'followed' (like following someone on Twitter) and can be visually mapped in terms of the amount of work that is done to them over a given period of time. GitHub is well known for hosting code rather than consumer-level, packaged programs. Almost 2 million projects are now hosted there, eight times as many as SourceForge.

Google Code and CodePlex

Google's repository is where you'll find Google's own code, of course, including snippets to develop projects for the Android or Chromium operating systems. Many other projects also use Google Code, as it offers hosting space and a reasonable range of support functions, although not as wide as GitHub.

CodePlex is Microsoft's equivalent, hosting and supporting open source projects for its own platforms such as SQL Server and Sharepoint. It is probably only of relevance to commercial developers that are focussed on these products, although the majority of Microsoft products are not, in themselves, open source.

Intellectual property

The way in which open source is offered is up to the developer. Licences are not absolutely necessary, but they are a good idea as they let consumers and producers know exactly what they can (and can't) do with a particular product. They are not designed to be restrictive per se, but rather to provide clarification in terms of use.

Open source and free materials are often bound up in a form of licencing called 'copyleft'. An obvious play on 'copyright', this is a concept which plays with standard practice in allowing people and organisations to modify the originating work, and to freely distribute it. Below are some examples of licences associated with open source, some copyleft, some not. There are many more, however these are the most popular and widely recognised.

Examples of open source licence types

GPL (GNU Public Licence)

The GPL is a copyleft licence. It is the most popular of all of the free and open source licences. It's from a project called GNU (a recursive acronym of 'GNU's Not Unix') which is supported by the Free Software Foundation, and offers a free operating system based on Unix. The GPL ensures that software remains free to use and to experiment with. Software can be modified, copied, and distributed, either as the original work or any derivative. However, whilst the software is free to use under the terms of the licence, a modified or new version may be offered at a price. The original producer of the code must therefore be comfortable that successive versions can make other people money.

BSD license (Berkeley Software Distribution)

The BSD license is not a copyleft licence, as it includes stricter enforcement on derivative works. BSD was a distribution of Unix that has now been superseded. The current, comprehensive version of the BSD licence, called the 'New BSD Licence', provides for an unlimited redistribution of the work, for any given purpose. The condition is that a copyright notice and a warranty is retained with the work, and that contributors to the work cannot be endorsed without their permission.

It is GPL-compatible, so it maintains the context and spirit of that licence. However, whilst catering for free distribution, the BSD licence allows for tighter control over how both the original and subsequent developers' reputations are managed.

http://en.wikipedia.org/wiki/BSD_license

EUPL (European Union Public Licence)

The EUPL is a coypleft licence. It has been approved by the European Union and, like the BSD licence, is GPL-compatible. The reason the EUPL was created was to ensure that European producers and developers have a licence that is compatible with European copyright law, since the GPL, BSD and others, due to their origin, are related to American law.

The EUPL has a canny relationship to other licences. If you release a work under the EUPL, you may also (re-) release it under the GPL. As you might expect, the EUPL has found favour with public organisations, especially those with a relationship to the EU itself. However, there is no reason why it cannot be used in any free and open source project. It is flexible, it is GPL-compatible, and is effectively guaranteed by the EU itself to be entirely compliant with European law. So, for anyone in Europe considering offering work that is free and open source, and encourages reuse, the EUPL is worth considering.

MIT Licence

The MIT (Massachusetts Institute of Technology) licence, like the BSD, is not a copyleft licence. It provides similar features to other licences and is, again, GPL-compatible. With the MIT licence, work may be distributed freely but the original producer remains in control of the Intellectual Property. This is therefore useful for any proprietary work – such as artistic works – that may be actively distributed but not permitted to be changed.

Material licencing

It is worth pointing out that although the origins of open source are very much in software, anything that has a material source can, in theory, be opened up in the same way. More and more sectors are looking to use the open source model as a way of offering material. Whereas software developers may offer code under the GPL, producers of material content, such as film and music, may offer content under a Creative Commons licence. The point to make regarding Creative Commons is that there are many licences available, and some are perhaps more in the spirit of open source than others, although there is no 'official' guide to the compatibility of Creative Commons licences with open source, and so it will always come down to individual and organisational approaches which one is appropriate to choose. In this, it mirrors the problematics of licencing more generally.

Participating in open source communities

If you're thinking of developing your own software, joining open source forums and communities is a great way to get involved. In such communities, people are there for the same reasons you are. They are keen to support the open source philosophy, they want to play a role in the development of software and they want to integrate this software into their own projects.

Many repositories host discussion forums and other networking services around each item of software. So, for example, SourceForge hosts an individual discussion forum for every item of code or software that it hosts. This means that you can ask questions, provide comments, or even suggest new features. Importantly, as part of an open source development community, you are able to inform developers about what does not work so well. If a piece of software doesn't run on a particular Linux distribution, then the developers and the wider community need to know about it, and to look at how issues can be fixed for the next version, or if a patch can be applied (a small piece of code that corrects a problem). If you assist with reporting, then you may be invited to test a later version in order to ensure that the software works correctly.

GitHub provides more advanced networking features, where it's possible to follow people and projects. This provides a great way to keep up to date with particular developments (following a similar trend to the Facebook Wall).

It is, of course, recommended that you look before you leap. By their definition, open source communities range from beginner forums to the more advanced communities which feature developers and programmers directly answering and addressing issues. If you are an end-user of open source software, it may be the case that there are managed forums which can answer a variety of questions relevant both to novice and to more advanced users.

The larger suppliers of software, such as Canonical (for Ubuntu Linux) provide such features to help those new to the product. They are places for practically anyone to congregate and to help each other share and resolve problems, while putting new ideas forward. Any network is only really as good as the sum of its constituent parts, and communities that encourage less familiar users to join are highly productive for all.

Open source communities generally adopt an egalitarian approach. Whether you're a producer or a consumer, everyone has a role to play, and the greater the input that you can provide to these communities, the more your contribution will be valued. You may find that open source communities will be grateful for the knowledge and skills that you can offer – whatever they are. Experience with video will, of course, be greatly appreciated by developers and communities centred on AV and editing tools. Experience with mobile technology, whether from a technical or usage perspective, will be helpful to many. Find what's relevant to you based on your knowledge and skills, and it will be greatly appreciated.

What these communities are not interested in is an irate consumer of the product. If a developer has spent many hours of their own time, probably for free, producing a new piece of code or software, only to find that someone has complained at length about its faults, then it is likely to be rather demoralising – not just for the developer, but for many in the community that have played their part in producing the eventual work. If there's a problem, then there is often a procedure ('Bugtracker') where issues can be reported.

Open Source Publishing (OSP)

OSP has been working with Open Source design tool sets since 2006, working on the principle that designers need to be able to design their own tools (e.g. FLOSS versions of Adobe tools or fonts). OSP have an ongoing relationship with coding communities such as the developers who work on Scribus (the FLOSS alternative to Indesign), as well as releasing many of their own Open Source font libraries.

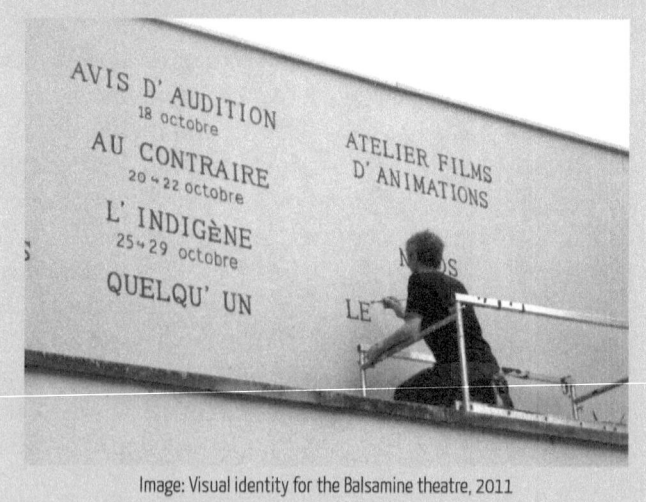

Image: Visual identity for the Balsamine theatre, 2011

http://ospublish.constantvzw.org/

Open source and your digital work

The continued development of artistic works that utilise digital media invites a greater level of openness of intellectual property than ever before. A structured, global approach to open content, open source and open licencing have all come from digital media, and it's easier than ever to open your work up for further development. If your work has been funded, then making your work open source is a great idea to add value and to build longevity after the funded project is over.

Making your work open source may be more of a philosophical and political than practical decision, since it doesn't require a lot of time or effort. By making work open source, you will ensure that others can share in the thought, research and developments that you have undertaken in order to produce your results. Of course, it is also worth mentioning that if you open up your source material (with a given licence, such as ECPL or GPL), and it is then modified and improved, you're free to take the improved code and continue to work on it yourself. So, if you have some code or materials that you cannot commit to improving, but you retain a vested interest, you may decide to become active once again after others have worked on it, by which time a community has built up around it.

Open source and your non-digital work

As the concepts and philosophies which underpin open source are consistent across any producer-consumer relationship, the opportunities to take open source out of computing into other practices and sectors are very much there. In applying the principles of open source outside of the digital space, producers and organisers have the opportunity to unlock a wealth of intellectually rigorous, valuable content which can be accessed, enjoyed and reproduced by the many, rather than the few. Open source has tremendous potential in education, and perhaps in marketing too, where opportunities to work with source material could lead to greater engagement from audiences, virtually or in situ.

Critical analysis of the potential of open source in art has been taking place for at least the last decade and it is fair to say that open source art will have a healthy future. Film in particular has made tremendous steps in adopting open source as a philosophy, even in feature film. Valkaama, for example, is a feature-length film from Finland which calls itself a 'collaborative, open source movie'. Released in 2010, the promotional website offers the entire film, as well as the script, the music and the credits, for download. Although all of this is available for free, there remains a commercial element, as the producers offer HD versions of the film for exhibition in cinemas, as well as sell DVDs and posters through the website.

5
Audio
Catching butterflies with copyright nets

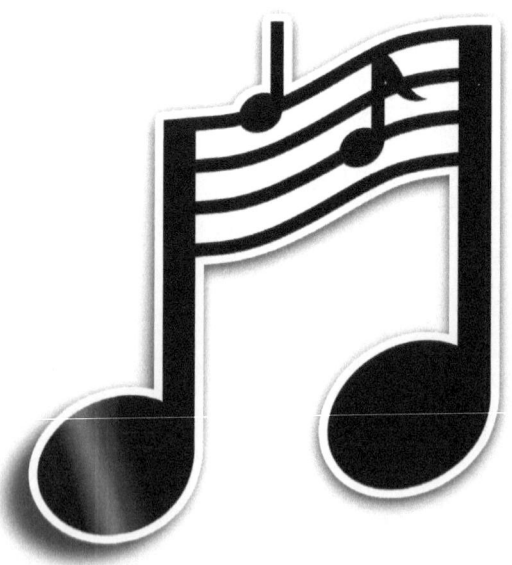

Digital audio is the transmission and reception of sound as data. The dominance of digital audio has been assured for around a quarter of a century now, since the invention of the Compact Disc, although it has changed significantly in the last 10 years. From 2000 onwards, physical forms of digital media have become increasingly obsolete, as internet bandwidth – the amount of data that can be transmitted and received – has continued to rise. This has led to an explosion in services offering audio either in MP3 form or to be streamed directly from the internet, as, for example, with the BBC's iPlayer.

Advances in technology have also given rise to new forms of listening device. MP3 players, such as the iPod, are easy to use and can store tracks by the thousand. Similarly, mobile phones and smartphones are becoming an increasingly important area of digital audio. To many, the mobile phone is now the main means by which audio is consumed and, in some cases even, recorded. Such is the ubiquity of these solid-state devices that portable CD players are becoming practically extinct.

So, for most producers, digital audio offers a number of advantages over preceding media. It's cheap to make good content, the content can be infinitely reworked and remixed and it can be offered in perpetuity. Storing audio in this way is also highly robust – the same sound is produced on every playback without degradation. As such, it is ideal for recording, distribution and playback.

Audio on the internet

Playing digital audio via a stream on the internet is usually handled by a plugin on the web browser. The most popular of these are Flash Player and QuickTime. The Flash plugin in particular is the means by which the majority of web services are offered, such as the BBC's iPlayer. This software is generally included with most web browsers, so that additional downloading is unnecessary.

Flash How To
http://www.adobe.com/support/flash/how/expert/interview/

Although the Flash plugin remains the dominant medium for playing audio through the internet for the time being, the advent of HTML5, the newest version of the HTML language used to produce web pages, means that a plugin is actually no longer necessary. Audio and video can be played directly in the browser. Although this may come as a relief to many as the lack of a plugin allows for smoother and faster performance, it can make offering audio more complicated. This is because although there is a standard specification for HTML5, different browsers will work with different sound formats. Most browsers will work with MP3, Ogg Vorbis, and WAV files, but other formats may be supported by a narrower range. It is therefore important to offer alternatives to HTML5 playback to ensure that a wider range of browsers can still play your content.

HTML5 Audio Support Checker
http://www.jplayer.org/HTML5.Audio.Support/

Much software is available so that audio can be replayed or broadcast over the internet without the need for a web browser at all. Audio players have become increasingly sophisticated in recent years. They can be synchronised with an MP3 player, so that audio files can be transferred, they can be used to stream audio through the internet and they can be used to download and listen to podcasts. It is likely that an audio player, such as Windows Media Player (WMP) or iTunes, will come pre-installed on your computer, but there are many more free audio players out there. VLC, for example, is a popular open source alternative which is available for all operating systems, and can play a wider variety of audio file formats than WMP and iTunes.

> VLC Player Download Link
> http://www.videolan.org/vlc/

As well as direct streaming, another popular means of listening to audio on the internet is through podcasts. These are media files, usually in MP3 format, which are distributed across the internet and are available as attachments as part of a data feed, which is normally based on the XML standard. A wide range of digital audio software now has the ability to automatically download and store podcasts, as well as synchronise them with a digital audio playing device. There are also many bespoke podcast clients (podcast catchers) available under free and open source licencing.

Although it is possible to develop a data feed manually, the vast majority of podcasts are available through an automatically generated feed. Websites with free and open source content management systems, such as Wordpress, Joomla and Drupal, are likely to have podcast features available, which make the publication of podcasts simple, so all the producer has to do is upload an audio file through the CMS. In addition, producers can and should make their podcasts available through directories. Many such services exist, allowing audiences to browse a wide and diverse range of audio content. Some of these directories also allow feedback from listeners, so it is possible to find out what your audience thinks of your content.

London Sinfonietta

London Sinfonietta has been making audio streams available for some time, covering works in progress to full performances. As an orchestra, London Sinfonietta supports its resident players, as well as commissioning new compositions and coordinating an extensive touring program. The streams act as a very important part of reaching new and existing audiences and encouraging people along to live performances.

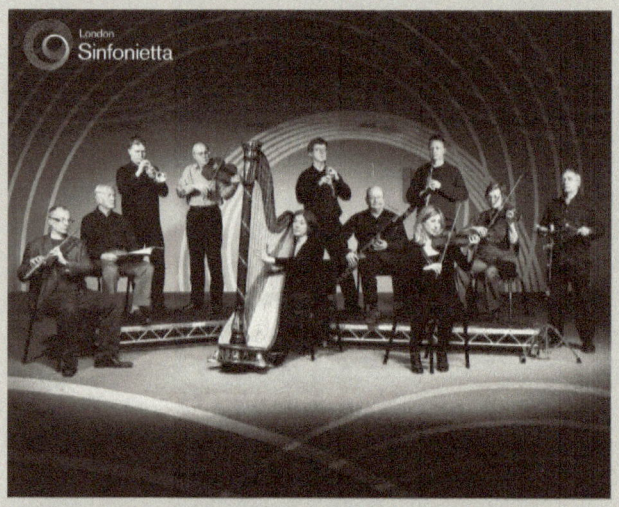

http://www.londonsinfonietta.org.uk/listen-watch-music-streams

Chord Punch

Chord Punch is a music label producing 'algorithmic music' (which it descri bes as "sound generated or inspired by automated processes"). Chord Punch is based in London and connected to its thriving live coding scene. Like many of its peers, Chord Punch uses the popular audio streaming service, Sound Cloud. Sound Cloud differentiates itself from other services in offering a well styled 'embed interface' as well as strong social media integration, through which users can comment on the timeline representation of audio files.

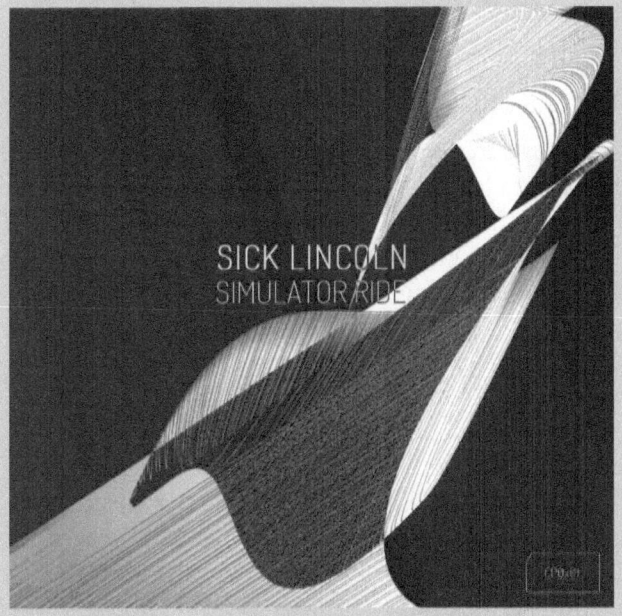

Image: Sick Lincoln

http://chordpunch.com/

Digital audio production

In digital audio software, sound is encoded into a file, and then decoded on playback. The programs that take care of this coding and decoding are known as codecs. There are many codecs available, which are often tied up with particular file formats. Codecs will offer different ways of compressing the data. Some are referred to as 'lossy' because the encoding process deliberately leaves out some of the audio so that the file remains small and therefore easier to distribute. Audio using lossy codecs will never be an exact replica of the original, although the quality will still be the same on every play. Some codecs, on the other hand, are called 'lossless' because they retain all of the original audio. These result in larger file sizes.

A codec is not a format. A codec is simply the way in which sound is encoded into, and decoded from, the originating file, and there are a number of codecs available for each format. By far the most popular format is MP3, originally developed by the Motion Picture Experts Group (MPEG). Although this format is flexible and highly popular, its intellectual property is protected by a patent. This is owned by the German research organisation Fraunhofer, which receives a royalty payment for the sale of every MP3.

Other proprietary formats are owned by commercial corporations. The two most well-known examples are Windows Media Audio (WMA), developed by Microsoft, and Advanced Audio Coding (AAC), developed by a consortium of organisations but known mostly for its use within iTunes. Software companies will inevitably promote formats and codecs endorsed or developed by them in their own software. However, the proprietary nature of these formats inevitably causes problems as, for example, it can be financially prohibitive for vendors to licence the necessary codec to play the audio. This means that certain formats are less likely to be playable on a wide range of players.

One open source option available is Ogg Vorbis. This format does not have any patents and is entirely open to use. Any organisation can use Ogg Vorbis in their hardware or software without entering into a commercial partnership. However, although this openness is a welcome alternative to the traditionally closed market of digital audio, it does not mean that all digital audio players and software will play it. So, again, if you're offering Ogg Vorbis, you may wish to consider it as part of a range of other formats for the time being.

The great benefit of this range of digital audio formats is that the level of fidelity (the quality of the signal) in audio recordings is entirely up to the producer. Fidelity is measured in digital audio as a sampling frequency, i.e. the number of times per second that a sample is made of the sound. This rate is measured in kilohertz (kHz). When CDs were the most popular format for digital audio, the sampling rate remained standard (at 44.1 kHZ) but as other digital audio formats have become popular rates have become increasingly diverse.

Formats aside, in regard to the editing and post-production of a digital audio recording there are many open source and commercial packages available. The professionalism and scale of these tools means that most producers will get by with popular software, without the need to spend a lot of money on more bespoke, specialist packages. One of the most popular tools is Audacity, an open source package which is available for free. Audacity offers a wide range of features for the recording, processing and output of digital audio across a range of formats, with effects including amplification and pitch change. It also provides multi-track functionality, so that you can produce a single piece of audio from a number of inputs (such as microphones or tape recorders), editing and synchronising them directly in the tool. Another handy function within Audacity is its capacity for re-sampling, so that audio recorded at one sample rate can be converted to another with minimal loss of quality and fidelity.

It is also possible to outsource the editing and production of your work to a third party. As is always the case with external providers, however, you should ask them for a reference, a sample of their work, and for their thoughts on how your audio can be brought to life online, and for it to be unique in an environment where audio is constantly available from a diverse range of broadcasters, producers, and artists.

Ogg Vorbis

Ogg Vorbis is the open standards audio codec designed as a replacement for MP3. This name is a little cryptic and worth unpacking just to get a peak inside the coder world from which it emerged. Ogg is the gaming term for forcibly squeezing something, while the word Vorbis is based on the 'Exquisitor Vorbis' character from Terry Pratchett's 1992 Discworld novel, Small Gods.

Sound artist Mattin uses the Ogg Vorbis audio file format for output from the music label, Free Software Series. Try it out via Archive.org, where you can upload existing audio files and have the site generate and host the Ogg Vorbis version, as well as a wide variety of other file formats. It also gives you a nifty embed player to put back on your site.

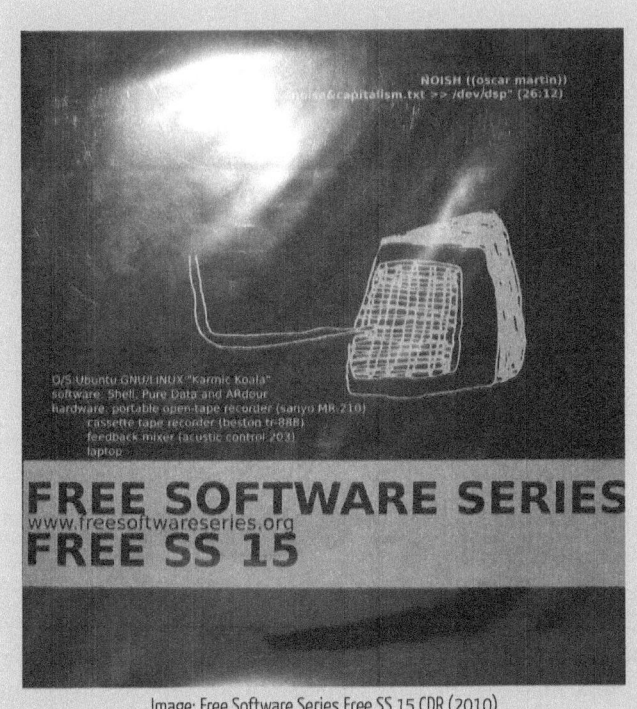

Image: Free Software Series Free SS 15 CDR (2010)

Free Software Series
http://www.freesoftwareseries.org/

About Ogg Vorbis & Frequently Asked Questions (FAQ)
http://www.xiph.org/xiphname (read down)
http://www.vorbis.com/faq

Recording audio

Music

As outlined above, music should be offered at a minimum sample rate of 44.1 kHz, unless you want to deliberately degrade the audio for your own purposes. Recording in stereo is also recommended, particularly if the recording is in an open space and/or you are producing for an audience that you anticipate will use personal digital media players. If you can, record with a number of microphones with a multi-track machine. However, if this is not possible, then do seek out the best possible microphone (or microphones) for recording.

Speech

The quality of a speech recording depends entirely on the recording hardware and environment. Speeches and recitals with more than one person involved should ideally use one microphone per person, recorded to a multi-track machine for subsequent post-production.

For a recording which is to be made on location, there is a wide range of equipment that can be used for recordings, from smartphones to professional portable recorders. However, it would be wise to let your listeners know about the recording quality before they listen to the work.

Theatrical performance

The recording of a theatrical performance requires a similar approach to that of music. Again, you should record at the best sampling rate available (minimum 44.1 kHz) and use good-quality equipment and microphones. A separate microphone per performer will achieve the best results, although if this is not possible, use as many good-quality microphones as you can.

A recorded performance may be wonderfully engaging, but recording a performance in front of an audience may result in poor sound quality unless it is well thought out. Make sure that the microphone equipment is situated in a location that allows for the recording of audience feedback, such as applause. It doesn't have to be loud, but it has to be recognisable.

Presenting your digital audio
Internet radio

There are an increasing number of community radio stations in the UK. Perhaps the most well-known radio station for artistic organisations is Resonance FM, although many more exist. Community and restricted-access stations are always keen to hear from contributors. If you consider there to be a fit between your content and the station, then please contact them. It doesn't matter if your content is a one-off, or a weekly podcast. Many stations will take a positive attitude to the submission of content, and will be happy for the publication of that content to co-exist on your own blog or website. If the relationship between your work and the radio station develops to the extent that it becomes regular, then remember to mention the radio broadcast during the recording itself.

Alternatively, you may wish set up your own radio station. This is a great way to stream audio. IceCast is an open source platform through which audio can be streamed across the internet. As long as you have a reliable broadband connection with good bandwidth, the software can send your content directly to an IceCast server, which allows the listener to connect to an Ogg Vorbis or MP3 file and to listen to it as a stream.

> IceCast Server
> http://www.icecast.org/

An even easier way to broadcast, which is less slick but still provides a streaming solution, is through Andromeda. This is a script which turns a set of MP3s into a small widget, where the MP3s can be played individually, or as one single audio stream. Although Andromeda isn't an elegant solution, it's easy, and may be an option for podcasters looking to add reach and ease-of-use to their content.

> Andromeda Streaming
> http://www.turnstyle.com/andromeda/

Publicising your audio

However regular your audio output, it must be prominently available from your website. One of the qualities of the BBC's iPlayer service, for example, is that it collects all the output from one organisation and makes it available in one place. Strategically, you may wish to consider doing the same, offering an audio microsite or sub-section within your website which offers unique content as well as detailed advice on how your audience can download, listen, and contribute. If you are going to offer regular content, such as a podcast, you should consider issuing an announcement (or a press release) to your contacts to launch the service. The announcement could feature an invitation for the intended audience to provide feedback or even record their own clips for inclusion in future features.

You should present your audio as a single production

per page, rather than simply offering a list of files. Whilst it may be more convenient to offer a list, this can be difficult and confusing for search engines to locate. For example, if you have a programme on a particular artist, and you dedicate a page to this, then search engines are much more likely to pick up that page when someone conducts a search by that artist's name. Such clarity also means the content is more likely to be linked to from other web pages, as many external authors and bloggers will link to the web page rather than the audio file itself.

Finally, ensure that your audio programming cross-references itself. If your audience is listening to your audio content, then they are engaged, so why not incorporate some publicity within the clip to inform them of other programmes? It's a simple way to build awareness, although you should avoid complex URLs where possible, because listeners may not always have an internet connection available, and will need to remember it. Keep spoken URLs succinct and easy to memorise – whether it's your URL or anyone else's.

Backdoor Broadcasting Company

Backdoor Broadcasting Company is an audio recording and online distribution service. You can get the Backdoor team to come to your organisation, record an event, and then edit and upload the result as a podcast or stream. Backdoor hosts an extensive archive of talks across a wide variety of artistic and academic fields. It primarily provides services to academic clients, but also works with a variety of artistic organisations.

http://backdoorbroadcasting.net/

To monitor the response to your content there are many free analytics tools that allow individual audio files to be tracked in terms of 'listens'. You should keep a regular eye on this and if it isn't climbing, you may wish to ask your audience what you can do to improve their experience. Their answers may be different to what you were expecting. For example, whilst there may be an assumption that the content needs improvement, their view may be that the content is fine, but the data feed is flaky and you are not offering sufficient regularly-updated files.

Commercial models

Many people and organisations offer high-quality audio content for free. Indeed, some of these organisations are amongst the world's largest media companies. However, if you are thinking of charging for content, then there are two main ways to do so. The first is pro-active (charging before the listener can receive it) and the second is reactive (asking for the listener to pay after a download).

Charging the listener to download a file is easily done. Many open source CMS platforms offer e-commerce plugins or services, meaning that products can be purchased online. As a digital download is effectively a product, the consumer can pay for their download and be given access to a page where they can download the audio file. An issue to be aware of here regards Digital Rights Management, and the question of if/how your audience should share your content. If one person pays and they share it with another 10 people, should those 10 people also have paid for it? If you believe they should then you will need to enable DRM in your sound files. DRM is usually available with proprietary formats.

Additional facets, such as providing a ceiling (where

the file expires after a given number of plays or time period) may also be considered. A way to make this easier is to effectively devolve the selling process to an external company – a digital distributor – who will sell your work on major audio stores on your behalf. They will charge a fixed fee and often a commission on each product sold. An upfront fee will also need to be paid to obtain a Universal Product Code.

Reactive payment is a good solution for producers who do not want the hassle of charging upfront, but still feel that their content has some degree of commercial value. One option here would be to ask for a donation. A producer may offer their content for free, but invite people to donate through a link on their website that takes the listener to a donation page (these are often provided through PayPal). Offering this service often signifies a mature relationship between listener and creator, whereby a willingness to offer interesting content is matched by a willingness to make a financial contribution to the creative process.

NMC Recordings & State51's Greedbag

NMC Recordings carries out the recording and distribution of what it describes as 'the best of contemporary music' which, for want of a better term, we might call contemporary compositional music. To see the extent of their repertoire it is worth checking out their fantastic music map, full of music clips, meticulously researched background information and visualisations of composer, genre and other relationships.

NMC uses the GreedBag audio e-commerce system operated by State51, the expert audio encoding company. It offers free samples to the web user and then paid downloads, including high quality FLAC files.

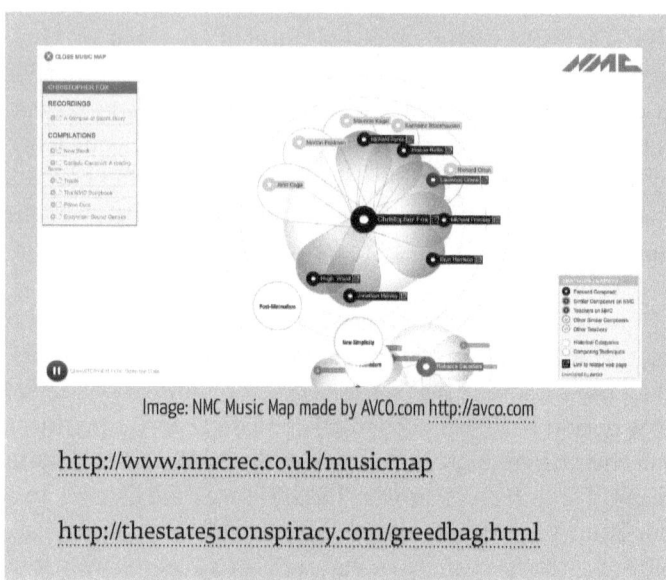

Image: NMC Music Map made by AVCO.com http://avco.com

http://www.nmcrec.co.uk/musicmap

http://thestate51conspiracy.com/greedbag.html

6
Gaming
Gaming as learning, gaming as culture, gaming as a new context

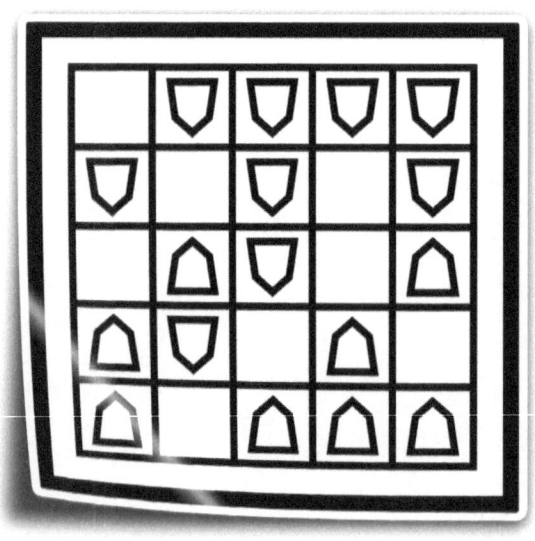

Gaming technology has come a very long way in a short space of time. Games are sophisticated, enormously diverse, and home consoles such as the Wii, PS3, and Xbox 360 have allowed them to incorporate phenomenal amounts of visual detail. The Wiimote (the controller for the Wii), Move and Kinect (the gestural systems for the PS3 and Xbox respectively) also allow a level of physical interaction previously unimaginable. All these things have been instrumental in taking gaming beyond the screen and into physical space.

In addition to consoles, smartphones represent a significant development in interactive gaming. They are packed with features that can enrich a physical experience, including location awareness and mapping, SMS and social networking. Many game producers now use specific mobile apps, whether as a game in themselves or as part of a wider game. The social networking website, Foursquare, for example, uses the GPS hardware in phones and an app to allow users to 'check in' with their current location, winning points every time they do so. They can become the 'Mayor' of a particular location, and share this information through Twitter and Facebook.

Chromaroma

Chromaroma is a game developed by Mudlark that tracks movements of registered passengers with their TFL Oyster card. By taking different routes and by working collaboratively with other 'players', points can be accrued. Through exploring the city in new ways and establishing new contacts, the act of travel itself becomes more exciting and the city an interesting place to explore, rather than simply a place for work and commerce.

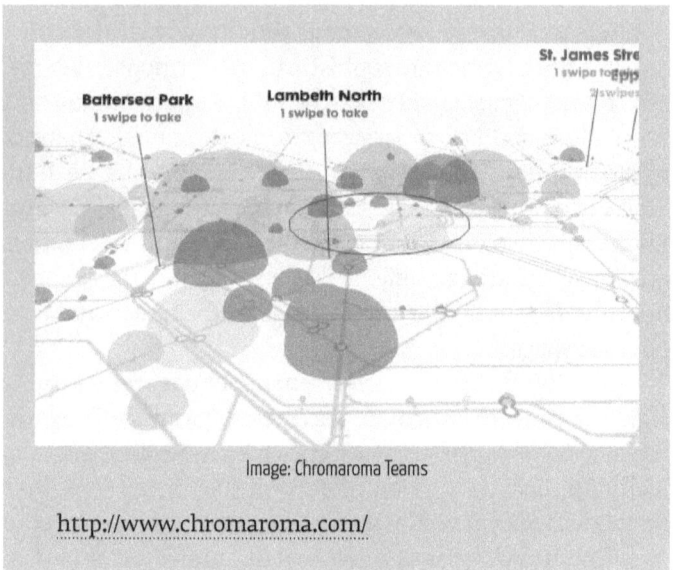

Image: Chromaroma Teams

http://www.chromaroma.com/

Another development involves the integration of multiple media within a single game. This is a concept known as transmedia. In such a game, the narrative may begin on a website, then move onto a mobile phone which receives an SMS to ask the player to perform a physical action 'in the real world', which then opens up a new level of the game. This kind of gameplay has tremendous potential to offer rich and complex narrative and allows the player to interact in a multitude of ways. As might be expected, this also means it is being used increasingly in advertising campaigns, from Old Spice to Audi.

Such developments have been made possible due to the increasing sophistication of technologies that can be used to support gaming. For example, QR (Quick Response) codes enable smartphone users to use an app to scan a barcode which brings up information in the phone's web browser. Examples of QR reading apps are QRdvark for Android, and NeoReader. QR codes allow for the direct mapping of a URL onto a graphic code for free, meaning that it's possible to make QR codes for any mobile or standard web page, and to print them out onto paper or sticky labels. Because QR codes link the physical world with the virtual one, they are ideal for games where there is a degree of physicality in the narrative. A good example would be a school 'treasure hunt' game, where groups have to find treasure based on the successive discovery of these codes. Similarly, SMS can be used to deliver clues 'spoken' by the character of a game. This works particularly well with live, mass-audience games.

Yet another development which is becoming increasingly popular and offers many possibilities is that of group gaming. In such games, which have become very popular online, participants can communicate with one another within the game itself and take on certain roles, either in competition with each other or in order to accomplish a shared goal. As we shall see, group gaming can have an extremely worthwhile application in education and outreach.

Before we go on to look at specific contexts in which a game might be developed, there is a more general point to consider which is applicable to all games, and concerns their rules. Bear in mind that many potential participants will search online for your game (whether it's fully digital or not) and will perhaps read commentary on it. If the comments criticise the game for it being too abstract or difficult to understand, you risk putting people off.

At the same time, however, you do not want to make the game too easy, and the rules and specific purpose of the game do not have to be given away all at once. They can be gradually revealed as the game unfolds. As we shall argue with regard to marketing campaigns, the capacity for the user to unlock new information as they go can help to maintain interest and engagement.

The point of rules is that they must invite the player into the world of the game. If the rules are too hard early on, then maybe only a few players will want to continue. Make it too easy, and it won't be inviting or challenging. But it also depends on the nature of the game itself. For example, simple games work when they are fun whilst more complex games work when they are emotionally powerful and intellectually challenging.

Artistic projects

Artistic works do not have to be games in themselves, but games can be one part of the work, or used in a way that complements the work. A sculpture may be accompanied by a game where participants have to assemble the sculpture on a computer screen or tablet. A short film may be accompanied with a game based on the characters. A writer may develop a game that provides a new way of looking and interacting with their original material. In other words, there are many opportunities for audiences to engage and interact with the art work and to experience it in a more direct way, which may increase its emotional resonance. With interactive gaming technology it is not necessary for them to see the hardware itself or even to use anything more than their body.

Games in an artistic context do not necessarily have to be visually exciting or use sophisticated technology. Some of the most interactive and physically interesting games will use simple LED displays, CCD cameras and old computers. That said, whether the game occurs in virtual space, physical space or in both, and whether the work itself is a game or is merely supported by it, careful planning will be required to determine, for example, how much assistance may be needed in its development and the anticipated demographic that will play.

A game that requires a certain physical environment can be immersive and visually rich. However, if your game has physical elements to it these may require additional equipment, such as sensors and displays. It may also require additional costs to build, transport and store. You may find it useful to talk with organisations that will host your work, such as galleries, as well as other producers of games with physical equipment prior to starting the build. If your game runs on popular hardware such as a PC, Wii, PS3 or Xbox, then the organisation may already have such equipment, or know where it can be obtained.

Irrespective of whether you are building a system or using someone else's, you should ensure that your work has a list of all requirements, from those within the base unit (e.g. 'PC with 1GB memory running Windows XP or later') to any specific peripherals (e.g. '2 joypads with motion sensor capability') to the dimensions of the unit housing or any additional space required. You should also be specific about any particular ambient requirements you may have, such as, for example, lighting or floorcovering.

Works which are site-specific present a particular set of challenges in order to create a fully immersive experience for the participant, which invites them to engage with the space itself as well as their own sense of physicality and their emotional involvement with gameplay. Ideally, there will be someone at the site who you can liaise with in order to ensure that your work is effectively installed and hosted. They will need specific information from you regarding storage, transit and assembly, particularly if the game has physical elements which require players to move around a space, whether using controllers or not.

Warmail

Warmail was an installation at the HTTP Gallery (now Furtherfield) by Jeremy Bailey. It is a game rather like the war-in-space games of the 1980s, such as Tempest and Asteroids, although now it can be played by groups. It works through people controlling shapes with lightstick controllers. The points of the shapes contain a letter of the alphabet and when the group move the shapes to their appropriate points in order to spell out words and sentences, an email is created and sent. It unites gaming and composition in a way which is collaborative and fun to explore.

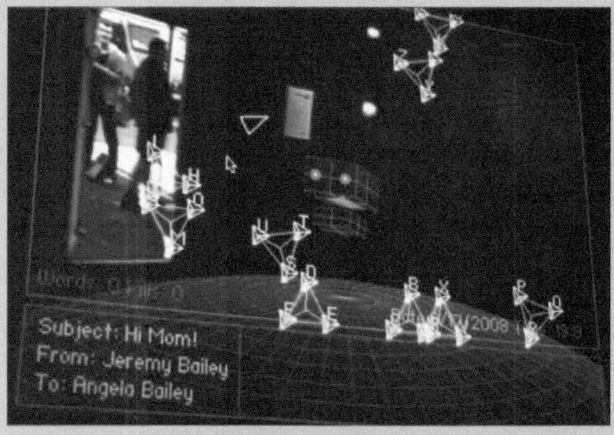

Image: Warmail

http://www.jeremybailey.net/warmail.html

Marketing campaigns

Since games involve an emotional engagement on the part of the player, they are ideal for incorporating into a marketing strategy. The success of a game as a marketing tool will depend on its narrative. Games and narrative are both based on progression. From Snakes and Ladders all the way through to Virtual Tennis, players advance through an environment and a successful game will create a narrative which is fun and engaging. One interesting and innovative way to tease the audience is to provide this narrative in separate stages, which are unlocked after the player has answered a specific question. For example, a gallery advertising a forthcoming exhibition may offer a QR code somewhere in the building, in a newspaper advert, or in a brochure. The QR code takes the visitor to a mobile web page, where they complete a simple task (such as a standard question and answer). Information is then unlocked which informs them of a new QR code that is available in the building at a certain place, on a certain date. The prize for completion could be an invitation to a private viewing. This kind of staggered narrative, based on participants undertaking simple tasks but playing a game that has a definite endpoint, has the benefit of being extremely cost-effective since mobile web pages are very cheap to produce, whilst QR codes are free.

There are, however, many marketing games that fail due to a lack of planning. To outline some of the potential problems and issues to consider, let's take as an example a marketing campaign for a film. In this case you might want a game which is related to a part of the film or to the characters within the film, and you may wish to offer it as a mobile app as well as something to be downloaded. While these attributes seem good on paper, there are many potential pitfalls.

It is important, firstly, that the game does not simply imitate a part of the film or the actions of a specific character as this would basically amount to nothing more than an expensive preview of the film. It should have some resonance beyond the film itself in order to maintain player's attention and encourage them to take part. The game could relate to some of the topics and concepts of the film and it could utilise some of the film's collateral, without directly referencing the film too much itself. This will help to ensure the game's longevity after the film has been watched.

Secondly, with regard to development, the game should not be developed for only one mobile platform since you want it to be available to a diverse audience. This means making it available across a number of devices, including iOS (iPhone), Android, and possibly BlackBerry too, which can make development extremely expensive. Obviously, making it available for download on a PC or Mac presents fewer problems, although, if doing this, remember that iOS devices do not contain a Flash viewer.

Education and Outreach programmes

Schools and communities offer tremendous possibilities for mass-participation gaming. Here, the producer has the opportunity to develop something that has an active audience. Also, as with gaming in artistic projects, since schools and communities offer the chance for interaction in physical spaces, there are many opportunities to combine digital and physical elements within the game itself. One of the main advantages of educational and community games is that they help to strengthen the ties between those involved, thus encouraging social interaction.

Although schoolchildren may appreciate a competitive

element, community projects may benefit instead from a gaming structure that promotes a more collaborative endeavour. It's also a good idea to consider endpoints so that children can be rewarded after a satisfactory conclusion, however it's possible for community games to utilise mechanics that take advantage of the network for collective play without such an endpoint, as demonstrated by Foursquare.

> **Tate Kids**
>
> The Tate Gallery's extensive collection of online games for under 16s provides ways for a younger audience to interact with specific areas of the gallery, such as the sculpture garden in 'Barbara's Garden', the Turner collection in 'Discovering Turner' and the building itself in 'Street Art'. These quick and simple games invite players to make certain choices in order to reveal outcomes, and to experiment with drawing and colour, whilst introducing them to artists' work.
>
> http://kids.tate.org.uk/games/

7
Community and Social Media

Opening the door to dynamic audiences

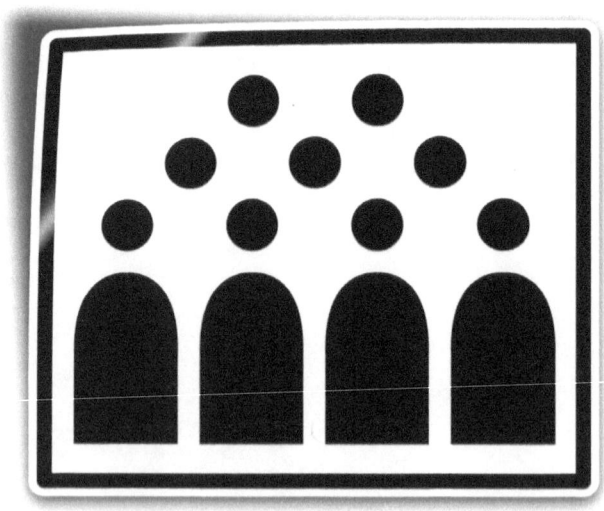

A potted history

Online communities have existed in a number of forms since the 1970s, beginning with bulletin boards (BBSes). These were text-based and used slow modem connections across the telephone system. BBSes remained popular throughout the 1980s and early 1990s as home computing became popular and inexpensive, allowing for wider access. As the systems that underpinned local BBSes increasingly gave way to the internet, communities started to become global. Because the internet provided a universal email system, email discussion lists started to play an important role in building online communities, making them simple, clear and easy for anyone wishing to join.

In the early 1990s, academic interest in the internet and online communities in general grew very rapidly. Many popular email discussion lists were run by academic LISTSERV (email discussion list service) systems, which were free for anyone to join irrespective of their affiliation to the host institution. This was joined by Usenet, an internet-based discussion and sharing service based around groups and topics of interest, often in very specific detail. As the volume of data on Usenet grew, it was clear that online communities were playing an important role in serving and supporting global groups with shared interests.

The continued growth of the internet through the mid-1990s and the explosion of low-cost connectivity allowed for further massive growth in community activity. Web-based discussion groups started to replace those using email and Usenet; these and other 'social technologies' evolved and came to be bracketed under rubrics such as 'social media' and web 2.0. As web functionality has continued to progress so too have 'social media' services such as Facebook and Twitter.

What are online communities good for?

Essentially, online communities are all about conversation: the giving and receiving of valuable, interesting and pertinent information and knowledge. This makes them particularly useful for group development, production and review, as well as for building awareness and engagement with your work or organisation.

Online communities can play a particularly radical role in the creation of new artistic work. Indeed, artists have worked within communities for centuries, either forming groups or movements themselves or having a group label given to them. Artists can form and work with online communities to help build their practice, to collaborate, to seek feedback on their work or to promote an upcoming performance. A community also makes it easier to find new participants for existing groups and collectives, helping to support ongoing work. To take one example of the value of online communities to artistic endeavour, the recent rebirth of jazz in the UK is in part due to individual musicians sharing audio clips and forming collectives, which has led to new albums and record deals.

A community provides fertile ground for experimentation and the testing of theories and ideas. Through collaboration, a piece of work is able to move in directions that may otherwise have never been explored. New forms, new styles, and new means of production and performance can be discussed, explored, and tested. It is also possible to experiment through the remixing of existing works. Producers can offer their work to a community in unfinished forms, asking participants to use it to produce new work. This principle could be applied in other fields too. For example, an academic may wish to share their research for collaborative purposes.

Online communities can also be used as an aid to

developing business strategy. They offer rapid and efficient ways to engage with stakeholders and other interest groups and to work through strategic consultation exercises at low cost, while building means of engagement way beyond the consultative period itself.

If, for example, a gallery wants to develop a new plan for local outreach, obviously management may still wish to hold face-to-face consultations with local groups and individuals, but this can be supported by the creation of an online discussion forum advertised through the gallery's website. The forum could be arranged into a series of questions, based on the relevant topics to be covered in the strategic plan, for example, 'How should artists engage with schools?', 'Do we offer the right mix of educational activities?', and so on. An indirect benefit of asking for such consultative feedback via an online forum is that the members of the forum can be easily retained after the consultation period has ended. This means that they can be used to monitor progress and developments whilst generally playing a more active and participatory role in the business or project.

Whatever they are used for, most successful online communities will have flat structures. This means that there is no 'leader' as such, although there may be a moderator to ensure discussion remains within agreed parameters. The point is that openly-accessible platforms with open communities are generally self-regulating. Dissenting voices, inappropriate behaviour, or spam can be easily dealt with by the community itself, provided it is strong, with a broad mix of participants.

But with this open, flat structure comes the question of ownership. Who owns the content in a discussion? Does it belong to the moderator, the participants, or to both? Does anyone even need to own it? Commercial social media services such as Facebook have clear guidelines regarding ownership. According to Facebook's terms, for example, 'you own all of the content and information you post on Facebook'. However, whilst Facebook doesn't own the messages on your screen, it does use the information to provide contextual advertising, displaying small ads based on automated scans of your content.

Whether you are establishing a community in order to solicit responses to your own work or to co-produce new work you may wish to consider how to manage this issue of ownership. It is important to cultivate a sense of shared ownership as you don't want people to feel that they are not in control of their own voices. If they are not, then they may not feel a strong enough sense of belonging to make a worthwhile contribution. You should therefore make it clear that everyone in the community expresses a personal view.

Some more issues to consider

The first decision you will have to make when cultivating your own online community is whether to develop and run the community yourself or alternatively outsource it to a third party. There are many businesses and agencies that specialise in online community development and social media. They can offer strategic input or they can manage the community on your behalf. The benefit of choosing this approach is the level of expertise that such an agency will (hopefully) bring to your project. You will find that the cost of such a service varies considerably so if you do decide to pursue this route, try to get a number of quotes (a minimum of three) and ask them to be very clear about what their offer involves. Remember that there is more to building an online community than simply using Facebook and Twitter, and if these are all they suggest it indicates a very narrow yet all too popular view that does not take into account the specific needs and desires of certain audiences and fails to understand where they congregate.

In the majority of cases there is no substitute for running your community in-house. It will be more authentic and you and/or your organisation will be seen to be more open and approachable. The trade-off, however, is the investment in time and energy that will be required – as well as, of course, expense. However, in terms of building personality and reputation, there's nothing like doing it yourself. If online communities and social media are about people, then it's in everyone's interest to make their own communities and groups as personable – and personal – as possible. That's not to suggest that you cannot solicit advice and assistance from elsewhere, of course. Similar organisations, people or groups should be called on to help to build an understanding of what does and doesn't work and what audiences appreciate.

The question of personality will also determine whether you choose to communicate as yourself individually or as your company or organisation. Company accounts are very common on Facebook, Twitter and on blogs. However, in all three cases you should make clear who the people are behind them. In the case of Twitter, for example, this can be done by adding a circumflex together with the initials of the person writing the tweet at the end ('Hi, we're just getting ready for our show tonight. Excited! ^AB').

In practice there is often considerable overlap between group and individual, for example when employees of an organisation are active individually on Twitter but are also perceived to be representing the organisation. The question to ask here is whether there is more value in communicating as an entire orchestra or through solos. Obviously, organisations with a high level of legal responsibility, such as theatres, cinemas and galleries, should consider carefully how their employees and stakeholders communicate in the context of the organisation. It is important not to be too heavy-handed in terms of what staff can and cannot say, because ultimately there is no way to contain it (they may simply create a pseudonym, which makes the situation much harder to manage). A better approach is simply to offer guidance and handy tips on what's good to say and what should not be said in public.

Most of us are aware that online communities involve a relaxation of individual identity. Indeed, in name at least, it is easy to become someone completely different. Having said that, personality comes across very strongly when you participate in a community so it is a good idea to think about how your particular traits might be perceived by others. This can be as simple as how you introduce yourself to people. It doesn't matter whether you are online as yourself, as a character, or as a group. How people engage with you is, in part, based on how you engage with them.

Managing communities, managing openness

One of the ironies of open, digital communities is that from the perspective of intellectual development, they are sometimes seen to be too open to be of use for concentrated thought. Whether you are planning to work with existing communities or create a new community yourself, you are advised to consider exactly how openness is framed. For example, whilst open, discursive conversations will take place, there will inevitably be times when a more direct and/or private approach is needed. Communicating your email address should help to attract private responses to any requests you make. It is possible to advertise your email address on social platforms such as Twitter, Facebook or blogs, but you may wish to consider an email alias in order to prevent spam.

In terms of managing the messages that come in, irrespective of how the community develops, you will need to have a moderation model. Here you have two main options, pre- or post-moderation. Pre-moderation means that messages require approval before being published, whereas with post-moderation any issues are dealt with after publication. Most services offer post-moderation, and this is the model which audiences are most familiar with. Pre-moderation used to be common in email discussion lists, although the overwhelming trend is now towards post-moderation, particularly with regard to comments on blogs and forums, and it is the only option on Twitter and Facebook. However, if you are dealing with highly sensitive topics with a controlled audience and you want to carefully manage the conversation, then you may find pre-moderation more appropriate. Of course, you will then need to spend more time approving and publishing messages within the moderation queue. Even if you do opt for post-moderation, you should ensure that members of the community are aware of how the moderation process is conducted.

Many email discussion lists operate according to a distributed model, meaning that members are free to talk about practically anything within the context of the list, and are encouraged to discuss and debate with each other. This collective way of working and debating is also apparent in web-based discussion forums, and is a great way to facilitate collective debate and development. A different approach would be the 'hub-and-spoke' model, in which the conversation is centred around, and emanates from, a particular individual or organisation. This is perhaps more valid for artists and arts organisations that want to create a group based around themselves, and is applicable to email lists and web forums, as well as Facebook and Twitter. Hub-and-spoke models lend themselves to more active moderation.

The point is that group activities require some sort of mutual balance, set either consciously or subconsciously. All roles within the community – moderator, active participant, or 'lurker' (someone who reads but does not contribute) – need to function harmoniously with one another. Key to developing this sense of balance is to provide context. If the group members know what they should be discussing, then it makes it easier to know when community development becomes unbalanced. Perhaps the easiest way to do this is to give a short explanation of what the community is for. This could be one short sentence, such as 'an email discussion list on technology and dance' or 'a Facebook group for film-makers in Lambeth', or it could be longer, providing more detail:

> A Google Group for players of woodwind instruments in London. You're welcome to join, whether you're new to woodwind, a recreational player, or a professional.

Where such a statement takes a slightly different form is on Twitter. Here, a Twitter hashtag creates automated groups based on the use of a persistent tag. If you are inviting people to discuss a specific topic with you on Twitter, then consider using a hashtag but try to restrict its relevance to your particular content. For example, don't use #art or #music as there will be hundreds of tweets using these hashtags worldwide. If you are asking people to respond to a request to participate in a community choir performance in Paddington, use something like #paddingtonchoir. Twitter does not provide the opportunity to describe the hashtag itself, so your original tweet should explain what it is about.

Another thing you may wish to consider in terms of managing your community is publishing a set of guidance notes and general house rules in terms of how the community should work. You will find considerable documentation available on this matter, the most well known being IBM's Social Media Guidelines document. However, it's best to create your own guidelines rather than copy others' verbatim, since the community will be based within your culture and it will be you who guides it. Of course, you should also avoid creating the impression that the community will be heavily regulated.

As part of your guidance, you will need to be clear about what will happen should certain issues arise. These can be anything from simply straying off-topic to the far more serious issue of online harassment and bullying. When it is obvious that you need to act on something, do so quickly. You will probably need to contact those involved, in which case keep a log of discussions. You may also wish to clarify to the community that an issue has occurred, in order to prepare them for any disruption that may result.

Identifying, building and retaining an audience

When launching your online community services you may wish to consider a Beta period, which in web parlance is shorthand for a service which is still under development. (It doesn't mean that it's rough. The photo sharing service Flickr was in Beta for a number of years, all the while accumulating hundreds of thousands of users.) What it means is that you are not formally launching, but rather testing and evaluating. It gives you the opportunity to take a sample of people who appear to be the likeliest to take part in your endeavour and invite them to the 'Beta community', giving them information on what you're asking them to contribute and who they can expect to communicate with (yourself and/or the group). If you are running something as amorphous as an email discussion list, blog or web forum, concentrate on one or two topics before it's opened out fully. It could be a discussion on your strategic plan, or a performance. Choosing a small number of topics will help you to quickly identify your Beta group.

As discussions develop in frequency and depth you can gradually open the Beta out in terms of people and topics, asking for volunteers along the way, until you are ready to formally open the service to your wider audience. From here, your community services – whether email, blogs, web forums, Facebook, Twitter or something else – should be available throughout your website. Ideally, there should be a short summary of recent activity, so new entrants to the community have a good understanding of conversation depth and frequency.

Communities often grow on the back of a particular activity, such as an exhibition, performance, or advertising campaign. The ability to maintain interest beyond this activity is critical. You don't want to see your community double in size around a performance, only to see it shrink back. As your community grows, grow with it, and grow your content with what they want to see or interact with. Over the medium to long term, your community may grow or it may shrink. One thing's for sure, it will most certainly change. In some cases, careful planning should allow you to adapt to whatever that change may be. For example, if you have anticipated a gradual increase, then it should be relatively easy to factor in additional commitments, in terms of time and resources, to ensure that it remains a success. However, not all communities work in such a gradual way. With Twitter, for example, you could have 50 followers one minute and then, on the strength of something you've said, have 100 the next, or, for that matter, 1000. One of the most powerful elements of Twitter is the retweet – the rebroadcast of a single message. If a message is retweeted many times, then it will be seen by more people, who in turn may be encouraged to follow. Some tweets will be retweeted, some won't. The point is that it can difficult to ascertain the effect your communication will have and the speed with which it will be noticed. It's therefore important to be flexible.

One possibility is to develop communities across multiple platforms. It is perfectly possible for people to congregate around different communities, and if you offer an email discussion list as well as a Facebook group, then different types of people desiring different outcomes will visit each one. For a performance venue, the email discussion list may be primarily for the artists or musicians, while the Facebook group would be for audiences. You don't have to cross-fertilise the two, unless there are specific benefits to be had from doing so. Two distinct audiences will not necessarily benefit from the sharing of content and discussions.

An old adage of social media strategy is to 'fish where the fish are'. According to this theory, rather than struggling to create your own conversation and community from scratch, you should instead participate in active, relevant conversations that are already taking place. There is an element of truth to this, but not in every case. Again, it all boils down to the strategic planning of your communities. But be aware that becoming involved in communities elsewhere requires an active level of participation that will still take time and effort. Part of this effort will be a great deal of listening. You will inevitably start by being one of the 'lurkers' before getting a feel for the best way to participate. Once again, planning is critical. You'll need to have a good idea as to which communities will provide the most value, will appreciate your contributions, and will be supportive of your endeavours.

www.ingramcontent.com/pod-product-compliance
Lightning Source LLC
Chambersburg PA
CBHW031429210526
45464CB00005B/2123